# First
# Beading

D0736298

CALGARY PUBLIC LIBRARY

JAN     2013

# First
# Beading

**Simple projects for beaders**

Jema Hewitt

COLLINS & BROWN

# Contents

Workshop
**17**

Art-Bead Pendant
Necklace
**28**

Bead Anklet
**30**

Name Bracelet
**32**

Pastel Seed Pearl
Bracelet
**34**

Cluster Earrings
**36**

Strand and
Art-Bead
Necklace
**38**

Vintage-Style
Tassel Earrings
**40**

Beaded Belt
**42**

Marcasite
Watchband
**44**

Starry Faux Lariat
**46**

Vintage-Style
Chandelier
Earrings
**52**

Beaded Hoop
Earrings
**54**

Night Sky
Memory-Wire
Bracelet
**56**

Scarab Choker
**58**

First published in the United Kingdom in 2011 by
Collins & Brown
10 Southcombe Street
London
W14 0RA

An imprint of Anova Books Company Ltd

Copyright © Collins & Brown 2011
Text and project copyright © Jema Hewitt 2011

This book was originally published as Complete Beading in 2004

Photography by Simon Clay

A CIP catalogue for this book is available from the British Library.

All rights reserved. No part of this publication may be reproduced, stored in
a retrieval system, or transmitted in any form or by any means electronic,
mechanical, photocopying, recording or otherwise, without the prior written
permission of the copyright owner. The patterns contained in this book and
the items created from them are for personal use only. Commercial use of
either the patterns or items made from them is strictly prohibited.

ISBN 978-1-84340-613-6

10 9 8 7 6 5 4 3

Reproduction by Mission Productions Ltd, Hong Kong
Printed and bound by 1010 Printing International Ltd, China

This book can be ordered direct from the publisher at
www.anovabooks.com

Vintage-Style
Rose Necklace
**61**

Leaf-and-Chain
Earrings
**64**

Feather
Chandelier
Earrings
**66**

Crystal Heart and
Pearl Necklace
**68**

Dragonfly Pin
**71**

Beaded Flower
Hairpins
**74**

Pre-Raphealite
Bracelet
**78**

Loomed
Swarovski Bracelet
**81**

Bead Woven
Choker
**84**

Fringed Bag
**90**

Cut-Velvet Scarf
**92**

Spiral Rope
Bracelet
**96**

Daisy Chain
Anklet
**99**

Buried Bugle-
Bead Necklace
**102**

Egyptian-Style
Netted Necklace
**104**

Netted Bead
Choker
**108**

Hemp Choker
**112**

Garnet Cross
**115**

Art Deco Bracelet
**118**

Frilled Peyote
Bracelet
**122**

# How to use this book

I have always been attracted like a magpie to anything that sparkles. In my youth, I loved the pots of sequins used by my mother to sew onto dance costumes, loving the way the beaded and bespangled garments came to life under the spotlight. It was a slippery slope – and I knew that one day my life would be filled to bursting with these delightful objects.

One of the loveliest things about beads is their longevity. If made from a high-quality substance, such as semiprecious stone or crystal, they will look as good hundreds of years from now as they do today. I love to rework necklaces worn by my mother and grandmother into new designs more suitable for me. It allows me to retain the memories of the beads but create something I will actually wear. Jewellery is no good in a box – it is there to be adapted and worn.

This book is divided into five chapters: Bead Threading, Wire Work, Looming, Embroidery and Bead Weaving. The projects range from those that are quick to make, to those that take time and require more skill. They are all explained in simple language and are designed to introduce just a few new techniques at a time, building up your confidence steadily and surely.

A comprehensive workshop section at the beginning of the book illustrates the basics, so you can see exactly what to do. Easy-to-follow text will teach you all the techniques you need to create the projects in the book. Each technique has a reference number, which is used for cross-referencing in the patterns.

The project section features 34 stylish pieces of jewellery for every occasion. Each one is accompanied by clear text and step-by-step photographs showing the key stages for easy reference as you work. The instructions for each project contain reference numbers, which direct you to the relevant technique in the Workshop, should you need to learn a new technique or be reminded of a familiar one.

# Beads

There are so many types and variations of beads that only the ones used within the projects of this book are described here. Part of the pleasure in creating with beads is experimentation, so don't be afraid to try substituting one size or type of bead for another – the results may pleasantly surprise you.

Seed beads are the tiny rounded beads used for the majority of bead-weaving and embroidery projects. They are formed when a long thin tube of glass is chopped into many tiny segments and then slightly melted again to soften their edges to create a rounded rather than tubular shape. Nowadays, they are mainly made in Czech Republic and India.

Seeds come in a bewildering variety of sizes, colours, and finishes, and, confusingly, the higher their size number the smaller the bead! This is because the size number refers to how many beads can fit along an inch. The primary colour of the bead is the colour of the glass from which the cane was made; different mineral additions, such as gold and copper, change the colours of the glass, creating rich hues. The finish of a bead refers to the final coating, which can make it iridescent, metallic, matte, pearlized, or silver-lined. The best-quality seeds are uniform in size and shape, and these are the ones you will need for most weaving and looming projects.

Miyuke Delicas are a more tubular version of the seed bead; they come from Japan and are almost perfectly identical in shape and size. They knit together to form practically seamless pieces of beaded cloth when used in peyote, brick, or looming. They are also very fine and light, so although 5g may not sound like a lot, you will get an awful lot of beads in a small packet. The variety of colours and finishes for these beads is extensive.

Bugle beads are long thin tubes also cut from canes of glass; they have many of the same finishes as seed beads and, additionally, can be twisted to form little spiralled tubes. Many bugles have very sharp edges that can cut through thread, so look carefully to check the suitability of each type for your project; Japanese bugles tend to have better rounded edges. Another good tip is to put a seed bead at the top and bottom of each bugle to protect the thread from fraying when used in fringes or bead-weaving projects.

Many beads referred to in stores as 'crystals' are, in fact, pressed glass. True crystal beads have a very high lead content in the glass from which they've been made, which increases their sparkle when cut. This adds to their price, but the obvious difference in quality makes them worth using whenever possible. The best-quality crystal beads come from Austria and are available in many sizes and faceted shapes. The most popular is the bicone, which is used in many projects in the book.

Pressed-glass and fire-polished beads are created by pouring molten glass into moulds. They do not have quite the same sparkle as crystal, but they are more readily available and much cheaper, with some lovely delicate iridescent colours in the ranges. They are often a nice oval shape and come in several different sizes. Italian glass beads are often created by millefiore canes. Millefiore means a thousand flowers, and that is just what these intricately patterned beads remind me of. To make them, tiny chunks are cut from a cane, which has a motif all the way through like a stick of rock, creating fascinating beads with lots of tiny pictures in them. Other Venetian beads have sparkling gold centres and a pretty raised-flower swirl. Venice was the centre for glass innovation in the Renaissance, and many skilled workers still create within the city, hand forming each bead over a torch lamp.

Lamp working is the process by which a cane of glass is melted over a hot-flamed torch and rolled around a thin metal rod to create a bead. The bead can then be further worked with the addition of other pieces of glass from fine rods called 'stringers,' pieces of millefiore, gold, and silver leaf. It can even be shaped into a whimsical figure or object. These beads often serve as a focal point for a necklace. The price depends on the complexity of the design and prestige of the artist. But when you consider the skill involved in its creation, the price paid for an expensive bead could be a bargain for what is in fact a miniature work of art. If you look closely at an unusual bead, thinking it is stone or lamp-worked glass, you may be surprised to find it is actually polymer clay. This fabulous substance can be used to mimic just about any technique of glass or finish of real stones without any special equipment. It starts out the same consistency as plastic modelling paste, and it remains pliable until baked in a regular oven. It is great fun to make your own beads with it, and excellent results can be had right from the beginning. There are several brands, each of which has its own advantages. Watch out for artists who work with polymer clay, too. They are making exquisite beads from this material that may become very collectible.

Metal beads can be either pure metals or plated. Pure silver and gold beads are often sold by weight, with the price of silver per gram changing according to market forces. Bali has long been a source of intricate silver beads, but be careful of the quality of the beads you buy. Silver comes in different degrees of purity – sterling silver has a high amount of silver particles within its makeup and will therefore be more expensive than a bead made from low-grade ore. Different countries also have different regulations as to what percentage of silver is acceptable before something may be labelled as 'silver.'

A wonderful product called silver clay has now made it possible to make your own silver beads, which you can mould by hand and fire using a blow torch. The silver particles meld together with the heat, leaving the clay part to be brushed off when the bead is cool.

Cloisonné beads have a metal base with wire soldered in patterns upon the bead; the different areas are then filled with collared enamel. This technique was applied in ancient Egypt using gold with glass melted into the spaces, but Chinese designs predominate today.

Many natural objects have been used as beads throughout history. Some of the first beads were pebbles with a hole that were found in prehistoric graves, so it is not surprising that bones, shells, and natural seeds all remain popular as components in jewellery. Found objects can always be drilled to add a hole – however many of these natural things are brittle, as I have discovered to my cost halfway through a project. So be aware of potential fracture points before drilling and threading. Bones, nuts, and wood can all be carved to create further shapes. Wooden beads may seem the province of only ethnic-inspired projects, but these beads can also be dyed and painted to create wonderful bases for embellishment by other beads or oven-baked clay.

Pearls are among the most precious found objects. The product of an irritation in the shell of the humble oyster, most pearls are now created by artificially inserting an irritant into shellfish farmed in vast beds in warm parts of the ocean. These irritants can be shaped so the object will be covered by the shiny nacre. Pearls were a popular wonder passed off as a natural miracle. It is also possible to remove the pearl without harming the shellfish, and this should be encouraged whenever possible in the interests of ecology.

As a natural product pearls are all unique – the most precious being perfectly round – but many shapes and shades will be found in a matching string. Fake pearls are made from glass, plastic covered, or clad with a pearl coating. Plastic and acrylic beads are a very affordable option for fun fashion projects, but pearlized coatings often do not last, and seam lines from the moulding process sometimes mar the larger beads.

There are many incredible colours and patterns contained within our rocks and minerals; the colour turquoise is named for a natural stone, even though it seems so far removed from the grey pebbles of most beaches. Beads made from semiprecious stones are just so beautiful, with their own inner glow. The choice of stones is huge; some are very expensive, some are surprisingly cheap. Semiprecious gems are often sold in long strands on temporary thread, but many shops will sell just a few of the more expensive beads. Before you buy, check the size of the drilled hole. Sometimes it's very small, and it can be frustrating to thread your lovely gems on a large hairpin! Different shapes are often available: round, square, faceted, and even little flowers, animals, and leaves can be collected.

There are different qualities of semiprecious gems, and stones also vary in colour. Amethyst can come in colours from palest lavender to very dark purple; lapis lazuli can be navy or bright blue. With experience, you will be able to distinguish finer gems from lower qualities. So long as the price is fair, always choose the gem most suitable in colour and shape for your project. Some stones need special care, so check with your dealer regarding how to clean and care for them.

If a gem seems to be too much of a bargain, chances are it is 'reconstituted.' These stones are made from dust and chips from the expensive stone, glued together with resin and reshaped. Coral and amber are often treated in this way, and many readymade jewellery pieces are reconstituted, while their labelling implies they are made of solid stone. Other gems may be dyed or heat-treated to enhance the colours. Howlite, in particular, is a popular base for a turquoise-colour dye. It can be just as lovely as the real thing, but it should be labelled properly.

# Tools and Materials

They say a bad workman blames his tools, but there are some pieces of equipment without which any beading work will be much trickier. There are huge storage systems for seeds and Delicas that allow you to see each colour. They are handy if you bead constantly or like to keep everything tidy, but I haven't found one necessary for my work. A small tool kit can be kept in a shoebox or an all-purpose plastic carrier, ready to be called into action when you want to bead. I'd hide it from the rest of the family, though, because the things you find most useful will inevitably disappear.

## Equipment

Small jewellery work pliers are essential for the neat finishing of jewellery pieces. There are several different types, and each fulfils a specific purpose. You can also buy three-in-one sets of pliers that incorporate the three main types in one tool. They are not as sturdy as separate tools, but they can be very handy if you like to travel with an in-progress project but don't want to carry everything with you.

**Round-nosed pliers** (top left) are used to create perfect circular loops. The pliers' tips are gradiated so you can make tiny loops or large ones. Among the many uses of these loops are attaching headpins to earring findings.

**Flat-nosed pliers** (top left) have a good gripping surface for holding small pieces while you work on them. They are essential for getting a firm hold when closing jump rings, and they make neat right-angle bends in wire.

**Wire cutters** (top centre) are the only things that should be used to snip any gauge of wire; even wire that seems as fine as thread will totally destroy your scissors. But don't use regular wire cutters on memory wire because it will chip the blades.

**Memory-wire cutters** are made from even stronger metal to cope with the added strength of this particular type of wire.

**Scissors** should be very sharp, because some strengthened threads can be awkward to cut neatly. A little pair of embroidery scissors is handy. Why not create a beaded string to hang around your neck so you don't lose them? Another method of trimming is by a tiny antique-style thread cutter. This is a very safe little object with a concealed round blade, but it will only handle fine threads.

**Needles** are another workbox essential. Flexible, large-eyed ones made from twisted wire are great for threading normal bead thread and thicker cords through medium and large beads. For seed beads, embroidery, looming, and weaving you will need a stiff, sharp needle. The eye is small, so only fine thread can be used with it. A needle threader won't go through either, so I have a handy magnifying glass, passed down through the family, which saves hours of threading frustration.

**Glue** is important for securing knots and attaching some findings. Cyanoacrylate dries fast and strong but also dries white, so don't get any on your beads! Specific branded bead glue takes a little longer to dry but is usually clear and strong. A dab of either of these glues is good for securing a knot. But in a pinch, a drop of clear nail polish will also do it.

Two-part epoxy glue is incredibly strong, dries clear, and is used to attach larger components together. It takes a little while to set after mixing, so you need to arrange the pieces to stay in position until then – try a bit of masking tape to hold them together. It will hold metal, glass, crystal, and wood, as well as other materials.

## Threads

Using the right thread will make or break a project, if you will excuse the phrase. There are many different types and even more different brands of each type, but you will soon find your own personal favourites and the ones most suited to your creations. Don't be afraid to try new threads, too; I have become a convert to several types after listening to a friend's recommendation.

**Conditioners**, which come in a little pot like a lip gloss, and traditional beeswax will strengthen threads, helping them resist tangles and remain strong. You just run the thread along the conditioner, from end to end, holding it firmly against the wax with your finger so every bit gets coated. Beeswax can make thread quite stiff, so do use it with caution.

**Nylon bead threads** are strong and used for both straightforward stringing and looming projects. Light and flexible, they come in skeins of many colours. Fine beading thread is used in bead-weaving projects when the thread has to pass through tiny seed beads or Delicas several times. It is stronger than sewing thread and easily threaded on a sharp needle.

**Plastic-coated metal wire** is extremely strong but can kink and bend in long lengths, so it is only suitable for straightforward stringing projects. Most types are too stiff to knot but can be crimped to secure clasps. There are many thicknesses and colours of plastic-coated wire with which to play.

**Monofilament**, nylon bead wire, and fishing wire are all-plastic threads. They are mainly used for intricate Japanese crystal weave projects and illusion necklaces, where tiny beads hang in swathes with no apparent thread to hold them. It is not suitable for basic threading but is often used on cheaper bracelets or necklaces sold to tourists. If you buy beads abroad, thread them as soon as possible to avoid breakages.

**Natural fibre cords** are an obvious choice for large natural beads and pendants. Thick cotton, hemp, silk, and leather all give a defined shape to a project. They can be knotted or braided to give texture, and there are faux versions of suede and leather, if you prefer. Cords may also be plaited or embellished with Chinese knots for extra texture.

**Wire** is not really suitable for the basic threading of beads. Wire is used for creating findings, such as eyepins and jump rings, and for special projects, such as tiaras. It is available in solid silver and gold, as well as plated metals. The gauge of a wire refers to its thickness in diameter and is usually measured in inches. Memory wire has been treated by heat so that it returns to its original rounded coil even when pulled out of shape. It is available in several different sizes for necklaces, rings, and bracelets.

**Chains** are also made by joining small links of wire together. Different styles of joining the links result in assorted patterns such as 'trace' and 'rope' chains. Most stores sell it by the inch for use in projects or you can just add a clasp and use the finished neck chain to hang a special pendant.

## Findings

Findings is the general phrase used for all those handy odds and ends that finish off a piece of jewellery. Very elaborate pieces are available, as well as classic shapes. Look for old or broken necklaces with lovely clasps or spacers; you can give a vintage finding a whole new lease on life with some fresh new beads, or a gorgeous clasp may finish off a great new design with style. Findings can be found in sterling silver and pure gold, as well as plated metals and some coloured steels.

**Headpins and eyepins** are essential for earrings and can also make useful components in necklaces. You can make eyepins very easily with a piece of 0.6mm wire and a loop made from round-nosed pliers, but headpins are best purchased ready-made. They look like dressmaking pins with no point and can be bought in an assortment of thicknesses and lengths, as well as assorted metals; some even have decorative heads.

**Necklace ends** are also called calottes and look like tiny clamshells. They are used to conceal the knot or end of a string and connect it to the clasp. They give a more professional finish than tying beads to a clasp with a visible knot. Thong ends are slightly larger and provide a neat finish for leather and thicker cords.

**Crimp beads** are tiny tubes of metal that are squashed on the end of a wire using flat pliers to hold the beads in place. They are often used inside a necklace end instead of a knot when threading plastic-coated metal wire.

**Jump rings** are tiny circles of wire used to join components together. They are available in different sizes, or you can make your own by winding wire around a knitting needle and then snipping down one side of the spring with wire cutters. Luckily, the rings will already be twisted open and be ready for your use.
I must admit that I get a bit carried away when I see unusual clasps, as they make so much difference to the final look of a piece. Some are just so gorgeous that I've used them as the central focal point as well as the fastening.

**T-bar clasps** are definitely a favourite for bracelets because they are easy to fasten with one hand. For the best security, it's hard to beat a simple lobster clasp. Both multiholed clasps and pretty cones are nice ways to combine multiple strands of a necklace down to one point for fastening.

**Spacer bars** keep different rows of beads separate from each other around the necklace. There are huge chunky bars that make bold statements and tiny thin ones you'd hardly know were there; some have holes placed far apart for big beads, and some are quite close. Check the distance between them to make sure your beads will sit in neat rows.

Because some people are allergic to base metal and can only wear pure gold or sterling silver through their ears, and others don't have pierced ears, it is just as well there are plenty of different types of earring wire available. The basic shape is that of a fish hook that goes through the ear. The bottom ring can be twisted open and shut to add a beaded headpin. There are many variations, including types for nonpierced ears, so find the ones that you think are most comfortable.

# Workshop

Use this section to learn the basic techniques you need to create the projects in this book. You can use many of them on their own to create simple items, but the Projects section shows how to combine several techniques to give detailed and interesting results. Here you will learn the skills needed for Bead Threading, Wire Work, Looming, Embroidery and Bead Weaving.

# 1 Necklace ends

**1** To close a crimp, hold it between the jaws of a pair of flat-nosed pliers and squeeze until it is flat.

OR

Tie a large knot, or even two or three knots, and then trim the ends.

**2** Thread on a necklace end, and close very gently with flat-nosed pliers around the crimp or knot.

# 2 Leather ends

**1** Place a dab of glue on the end of the cord; then close each side of the clamp one after another with flat-nosed pliers.

# 3 Headpin loop

**1** Grip the round-nosed pliers about 2.5cm (1in.) from the top of the wire.

**2** Twist the pliers through 90 degrees away from you, creating a right angle.

**3** With your free hand, curve the top piece of wire back towards you, shaping it tightly over the top of the pliers.

**4** Keep curving until the top piece crosses the other piece of wire, and remove the round-nosed pliers.

**5** Slide the wire cutters inside the **loop** so that the cutting edge is flush with the inside of the wire circle, and snip.

**4** Keep curving until it crosses the other piece of wire, and remove the round-nosed pliers.

## 4 Wrapped loop

**1** Grip the round-nosed pliers about 2.5cm (1in) from the top of the wire.

**5** Grip the loop with flat-nosed pliers.

**2** Twist the pliers through 90 degrees away from you, creating a right angle.

**6** Start wrapping the tail around the stem wire very neatly.

**7** Wrap three times, and close together.

**3** With your free hand, curve the top piece of wire back towards you, shaping it tightly over the top of the pliers.

**8** Snip close to the stem.

## **5** Opening and closing jump ring

**1** Hold each side of the ring with pliers, and twist. Do not pull apart, or it will not return to a perfect circle.

**2** To close, grip each side with pliers and twist back again.

## **6** Knots
### Square or reef knot (for two ends)

**1** Cross the left-hand thread over the right-hand thread, and wrap right around.

**2** Cross the right-hand thread over the left-hand thread. Pull up through the hole. Tighten the knot.

### Surgeon's knot (for two ends)

**1** Cross the left-hand thread over the right-hand thread, and wrap right around.

**2** Now cross the right-hand thread over the left-hand thread, and pull up through the hole.

**3** Wrap underneath, and pull up through the hole again.

## Overhand (for one end)

**1** Make a loop with the thread; curve the thread around; pass back through the loop. Pull tight.

### **7** Stopper bead

**2** Pass the thread over the loom, matching the gaps in the springs or slots.

**1** Thread on a small bead using a needle from right to left, and pass the needle back through the bead from right to left again, creating a loop.

**2** Repeat once or twice for a firmer stop; be careful not to pass the needle through the thread, just the bead.

**3** Wrap thread around the screw or hook on the other side, keeping the tension very firm.

### **8** Setting up the bead loom

There are many different models of loom so refer to your manufacturer's instructions for further details.

**1** Tie one end of your thread through the hole or to the screw, or hook on one side of the loom.

**4** Pass the thread back over the loom, going between the next space in the spring or slots.

**5** Continue until you have the correct quantity of threads, and tie off the last warp thread at the nearest hole, hook, or screw.

## 9 Starting thread and finishing off

**1** To start off, tie the thread on to the left-hand outside warp with a secure knot. Leave a long tail.

**2** To finish, tie a knot around the warp; then pass the needle up through the line of beads. Pass the needle down the next row, up the next, then trim. Repeat with the tail from the start of the thread.

## 10 Basic Weaving

**1** Thread on all the beads in the first row of the pattern in order, reading from left to right. Pass the needle under the warp threads, placing the beads so each sits between two threads.

**2** Support the beads carefully along your finger, and thread the needle back through the beads from right to left but passing the thread over the top of the warp threads. Pull the thread all the way through the beads.

## 11 Adding thread to a loom

**1** To add thread halfway through a project, weave the new tail back and forth through the loomed beads, exiting the last row in the proper direction for adding another line of beads.

## 12 Starting embroidery thread

**1** Make a couple of tiny stitches through the fabric, on top of each other, exactly underneath where your first bead is to be placed.

## 13 Finishing embroidery thread

**1** Bring the thread to the back of the work and take a couple of tiny stitches through the fabric, on top of each other, exactly under where your last bead has been sewn on.

## 14 To couch beads

**1** You will need two sharp needles and thread. Secure both threads to the material and thread on the beads.

**2** With the second needle and thread, start tying down every third or fourth bead by passing the needle over the beaded thread to a spot directly opposite and making a stitch.

## 15 Beaded back stitch

**1** Attach thread securely using a sharp beading needle. Place a bead on the needle, and push down to the fabric.

**2** Make a backstitch, bringing the needle point up where you want the next bead to be. Add a bead, and repeat the back stitch. You can place the beads as close or far apart as you wish.

## 16 Fringing

**1** Thread a sharp beading needle with plenty of thread, and attach firmly to fabric. Pick up as many beads as you need to make the fringe the correct length.

**2** Use the bottom bead as a 'turning' bead, and pass the needle back up through the fringe. Make a stitch at the top.

## 17 Netting

Different numbers of beads can be used in each netted piece; these are instructions for a three-bead netting pattern.

**1** Fasten on a stopper bead; then thread on a bead of the first colour (A), three of the second colour (B), one A, three Bs, and so on to the length of your piece, ending with an A bead.

**2** Thread on one B, one A, and one B, and pass the needle through the A bead of the first row. Repeat this sequence back down the row.

**3** At the end add two Bs, one A, and one B, and pass the needle through the A bead of the second row. Continue to the end of the row with one A, one B, and one A. Repeat from step 2 as necessary.

## 18 Spiral rope

**1** Thread a sharp beading needle with a length of thread. Place a stopper bead on the end of the thread by looping back through the bead. Thread on four size 10 seed beads for the core (A), then three in a contrasting colour (B). Thread the needle back up through the four A beads, creating a loop.

**2** Thread on one A bead and three Bs. Pass the needle up through the top four A beads, leaving out the bottom one.

**3** Repeat step 2, making sure your outside beads always lie either to the right or the left of the previous row, or it will not build up the spiral properly. Continue until you have a rope the right length.

## 19 Peyote stitch

Peyote stitch can be created as even or odd count and can be flat or in a tube. These instructions are for flat even count peyote.

**1** Thread a sharp beading needle with a length of fine beading thread. Place a stopper bead on the end of the thread by looping back through the bead. Thread an even number of contrasting beads in the pattern A, B, A, B, A, B, A, B, to the right width of your piece.

**2** Add another bead, B, and pass the needle back down through the next to last bead, an A. Add another B bead and missing the next B bead along pass the needle once more through the A bead. Repeat all the way down the row.

**3** To make third row, pick up an A bead, and pass needle through B bead. Repeat up row, picking up A beads and going through Bs, keeping tension firm. Continue from step 2 until it is the right size.

## 20 Attaching a thread

**1** When you have about 7.5cm (3in.) of thread left, cut a new length and tie a square or surgeon's knot close to the beads.
**2** Weave the end threads up and down in a zigzag pattern back through the work till secure; then trim.

## 21 Finishing the thread

**1** Weave the end thread up and down in a zigzag pattern back through the work, and when totally secure, trim close to the beads.

# Bead Threading

There is nothing more beautiful than a length of gorgeous beads simply threaded either as a single strand or multiple strands of cascading pieces. My philosophy is, why create complicated woven pieces when you can let the lovely beads do the work? So long as you choose good-quality beads and the right thread for them, your creation will give you pleasure for many years.

# Art-Bead Pendant Necklace

This gorgeous pendant caught my eye immediately, reminding me of a butterfly wing with its iridescent sheen. While toying with different design ideas, I eventually decided I wanted to keep the setting simple so as not to detract from the pendant. I also wanted to reflect the horizontal lines patterning the glass. The faux suede provides a nice matte texture that contrasts beautifully with the extreme sheen of the glass and the lines of Delicas. The pendant itself was made from fused dichroic glass by glass artist Jan Wilcox.

## You will need

Fused-glass pendant

Faux-suede strips in lengths of 43, 50 and 55cm (17, 20, and 22in.)

Plastic-coated metal wire in lengths of 46, 48 and 54cm (18, 19 and 21in.)

7g (¼oz) each of three colours of Delica beads

Two necklace ends

Five crimps

Two coiled-leather ends

Three 5mm jump rings

Lobster clasp

Flat-nosed pliers

Round-nosed pliers

Wire cutters

Glue

**3** Carefully hold all three threaded ends level; keep your fingers gripping tightly above the beads; and snip off the crimp with wire cutters. Carefully thread the three wires through the other necklace end, and finish with a crimp as before. Shut the necklace end, and close its loop.

**4** Place the ends of the three suede strips in the leather finding. With a pair of flat-nosed pliers, squeeze the bottom coil of the wire until it grips the suede very tightly. Thread the pendant onto the longest piece of suede, and finish all three pieces, as before, on the other side using the second leather end.

**1** Thread the three pieces of plastic-coated metal wire through the necklace end, and then pass them through a crimp. With the flat-nosed pliers, crush the crimp and close the **necklace end** 1 . Close the top loop of the calotte with round-nosed pliers.

**2** Thread each length of plastic-coated metal wire with a different colour of Delica; keep threading them on, all the way up to 2.5cm (1in.) from the wire's end. Place and crush a crimp on the very tip of each length as you finish, so the beads don't all fall off while you are threading the others.

**5** Open a **jump ring** 5 and thread on one of the leather ends, a calotte end, and a lobster clasp. Repeat on the other side, but include a second jump ring instead of the lobster clasp.

# Bead Anklet

The understated elegance of this charming anklet comes from carefully choosing a palette of contrasting but pleasing small glass beads from which to thread.

To make a palette of beads, take a little clear pot and start putting a selection of four or five of each bead in it. Choose two shades within your colour scheme, such as lavender and plum. Although both of these might be considered purple, they are different, in fact. Stick to beads that fall within those two shades. Keep checking your blend, and take out any beads that look unpleasant. You now have a beautiful selection from which to paint your thread.

## You will need

Silver T-bar clasp

Two silver crimps

Two silver necklace ends or calottes

33cm (13in.) of 0.015mm plastic-coated metal wire

Approximately 27 x 4mm beads and crystals of
assorted shapes

Approximately 27 x 5mm beads and crystals of
assorted shapes

Flat-nosed pliers

Round-nosed pliers

Wire cutters

**1** First thread a **crimp** ▮**1** onto the end of the plastic-coated metal wire, and gently squeeze with the pliers. Make sure it grips firmly and will not move.

**2** Thread on a calotte to cup the crimp like a pearl in an oyster shell. Very gently, close the **necklace end** ▮**1** with flat-nosed pliers.

**3** Thread on all the beads in a random pattern, but try to make sure no identical colours or shapes are next to each other. Get a nice mix of the two shades, but don't feel they have to be alternate.

**4** Check the length of the anklet, and add or subtract beads as necessary. Remember: there will be an extra 1cm (½in.) on the length from the addition of the clasp.

**5** Thread on the calotte and the crimp. With the tips of your pliers, crush the crimp leaving a ¼in. (5mm) gap between it and the last bead so the anklet hangs properly. Snip off any leftover wire with a pair of wire cutters. Close the calotte gently once more.

**6** Attach the clasp by gently closing the necklace-end attachment with a pair of round-nosed pliers.

# Name Bracelet

When a friend brought me these roses and leaves beads back from New York, I immediately thought of my mother, whose name is Dorothy Rose. I was taken back to my childhood and could almost smell the huge pink climbing roses that bloomed at the windows every June. So I designed a bracelet just for her. These bead roses climb up memory wire, a useful material that not only expands to fit most wrists but also needs no clasp to fasten it.

## You will need

Four coils of memory wire

Two headpins

Seven round rose beads

Square sterling-silver name beads

10 glass leaves

Nine 2.5cm (1in.) curved spacing beads

Approximately 30 small gold beads

Approximately 10 peridot tumble chips

Six small frosted flowers

Two large frosted flowers

Two pink hearts

Two 5mm pink crystals

Two 5mm red crystals

Six 4mm red fire-polished beads

Memory-wire cutters

Flat-nosed pliers

Round-nosed pliers

Wire cutters

**3** Make another loop at the end of the bracelet with a pair of round-nosed pliers, snipping off any excess memory wire before you start.

**1** Grip the very end of one piece of memory wire with a pair of round-nosed pliers, and curve it upwards. It will be very stiff, but try and make a complete tiny round loop. Put aside four tumble chips, four gold beads, two round rose beads, two small flowers, and two red fire-polished beads.

**4** Take the beads you had put aside earlier, and thread them onto each of the headpins with a gold bead, fire-polished, flower, gold, peridot, round rose, and another peridot. **Make a loop 3** but don't trim the end.

**2** Now place a gold bead on each end of the curved spacing bead and a leaf on each side of the round rose bead. Push the beads down to the end of the wire. Thread a gold bead between each letter bead, and create symmetrical clusters with the frosted flowers, crystals, and tumble chips. Keep threading until you have only 1cm (½in.) left on the memory wire.

**5** To finish off the dangles, hook the loop from the headpin into a memory wire end loop and **make a wrap 4**.

# Pastel Seed Pearl Bracelet

Pearls always look luxurious, and these dyed seed pearls have a chic contemporary feeling, as well. They remind me of the beautiful coloured puffed rice cakes I ate as a child. All sorts of colours are available, usually with a glorious iridescent sheen. I loved the way they looked in a heap together so I decided to strand loads together just for fun. Knotting between every bead is usually done with expensive stones to avoid loss if the string breaks and they all tumble off. It is also a neat and secure way to add French wire to the end of a strand. This wire, otherwise known as gimp, protects the thread from wear and gives a professional finish.

## You will need

Two 40cm (16in.) strands of coloured rice pearls
12 x 1cm (½in.) silver gimp/French wire
Five 3mm crystals to match pearls
Seven 4mm crystals to match pearls
Three strand silver clasp
Strong nylon bead thread
Sharp needle
Scissors

**1** Cut 50cm (20in.) of thread, and make two **knots** **6** about 7.5cm (3in.) from the end of the thread.

**2** Thread a long sharp needle with this length. Thread on three pearls and a piece of gimp. Next, thread through one of the holes in the clasp, and pass the needle down through the first pearl.

**5** To finish the other side, thread on a piece of gimp and the other end of the clasp. Thread the needle back down through the last pearl.

**3** Make a knot around the thread between the two pearls, and pull it tight. It should be large enough so the pearl can't pass over it but small enough to look neat. Thread down through the next pearl, and make another knot.

**6** Make a knot, and pass the needle down through the next pearl along; knot; thread down; and knot. Finally thread down through three or four more pearls. Trim the end of the thread.

**7** Returning to the loose thread on the other side, thread it down through three or four pearls, and trim the end. Repeat the stringing six times, placing two strands of pearls through each hole of the clasp.

**4** Thread the needle through the final pearl; make a knot over the first knots; and thread on the rest of the pearls, interspersing them with the occasional crystal (of either size) until you have the right length for the bracelet.

# Cluster Earrings

While I admit the 1950s may not have been a wonderful time for women's liberation, I just adore the clothes and accessories. Picture the perfect little woman, bustling around the home looking pretty in pastels. If you feel a more sophisticated look is for you, team these earrings with a chiffon scarf wrapped around in movie-star style and the classic Monroe sunglasses. Perforated findings are often used in vintage jewellery to create huge clusters of beads in a neat and secure fitting.
If you'd like to make a matching set, look for them to create necklace clasps and brooches using the same pattern.

## You will need

24 x 4mm crystals

12 Delica beads

12 freshwater pearls

Two 50cm (20in.) of nylon fishing wire

Two perforated findings

Two clips on backs

Scissors

Flat-nosed pliers

Glue

**1** Thread a length of nylon through the centre hole of a perforated finding; leave a 5cm (2in.) tail at the back to tie off later. On the front end, thread on a crystal and a Delica. Go back through the crystal, and pass the thread through a different hole. Make sure you hold the thread securely as you work to stop the ends slipping back from the holes.

**2** Bring the nylon up through the next hole; repeat the threading pattern; and take the nylon back down through the centre hole. Pull firmly to sit the crystal nicely against the finding.

**4** Thread on alternate pearls, crystals and Delicas, using the edge holes of the finding. Thread this pattern all the way round the central cluster, ending by threading the wire to the back of the finding.

**5** Tie off the nylon at the back with a **square knot** **6** and put a dab of glue on the knot. Trim off any extra length.

**3** Repeat this threading pattern until there is a cluster of six crystals in the centre.

**6** Place the finding onto the earring back finding and close the little flaps gently shut with pliers to secure the pieces together. Now make a second for a matching pair.

# Strand and Art-Bead Necklace

These gorgeous silver-lined glass beads have been acid-etched to give them a dreamy matte sheen. Because they are flat, they are not bulky when worn despite their large size. The colours are so subtle within the beads, I thought they'd get lost if strung with other large beads. So I used many strands of tiny seeds and Delicas to give a soft and subtle edge to the necklace. I was particularly pleased with the cylinder end beads that I tried in desperation after deciding all my cones were just too big. They do a fine job of hiding all the thread ends, while looking very attractive.

## You will need

Fine nylon thread

Thread conditioner or beeswax

Bali silver clasp

Two large cylindrical beads or cones that match the clasp

Two 7.5cm (3in.) lengths of 0.6mm wire

Three 2cm (¾in.) art beads

Six 5mm crystals

7g (¼oz) each of four colour-coordinated seeds and bugles

Needle

Scissors

Flat-nosed pliers

Round-nosed pliers

Wire cutters

Glue

**1** Cut about 63cm (25in.) of the thread and rub it through the conditioner to give it extra strength. Thread up the needle and place a firm **stopper bead** 7 7.5cm (3in.) from the end.

**2** Thread on 9cm (3½in.) of your first colour of small beads, then thread on a crystal, an art bead, a crystal, and then 6.5cm (2½in.) of small beads. Repeat from the first crystal and finish with another crystal, art bead, and crystal.

**3** Finally, thread on another 9cm (3½in.) of beads, and finish off the string with a very firm stopper bead. Trim the end of the thread to 7.5cm (3in.). Repeat the sequence from step 1 with another colour of seed bead, passing the needle through the same crystals and art beads that are strung on the first thread. Don't count the number of seed beads because they will be slightly different sizes – rely on your measurements to keep the seed parts similar lengths.

**4** When all nine strands are threaded, gather one set of end threads and carefully tie them all together very close to the beads. Repeat on the other end.

**5** Create a **wrapped loop** 4 with the 0.6mm wire. Pass the thread ends through the eye, and tie firmly. Place some bead glue on the knot, and when it is dry, trim the ends.

**6** Thread the eyepin up through a cylindrical bead, and create a nice neat **loop** 3 at the top.

**7** Thread one end of the clasp through the loop, and create the wrapped section. Repeat from step 5 on the other side to complete the clasp sections.

# Vintage-Style Tassel Earrings

In the 1920s, when women cut their hair for the first time into the short bobbed style, long tassel earrings were much in demand. The designer Erté used long-beaded tassels extensively in his couture dress designs for the rich and famous ladies of the jazz age. The long strings of tiny beads rippled and sparkled as these sirens danced their way through the tango and foxtrot, reflecting the movement. These tassels are not incredibly long, but feel free to create a more dramatic earring tassel of 4 or even 6 inches if you dare!

## You will need

12 x 4mm crystals

Two 2cm (¾in.) silver cones

Two 4mm round semiprecious beads

Four bead caps

25g (1oz) of seed beads in three varieties

Two 5cm (2in.) lengths of 0.2mm silver wire

Two fish hooks

Fine nylon thread

Thread conditioner

Flat-nosed pliers

Round-nosed pliers

Wire cutters

Needle

Scissors

1 With one length of the 0.2mm wire, make a neat **wrapped loop** **4**.

2 Now cut a 77cm (30in.) length of nylon thread, and pass it through the conditioner to strengthen it. Thread one end of it through the wire loop, and make a **square knot** **6** to secure.

5 On the final strand, wrap the thread through the wire loop several times and tie off with a knot. Trim the end to ¼in. (5mm).

3 To make the tassel, thread on 5cm (2in.) of seed beads and put a crystal at the bottom. Add a seed bead, which will act as a **stop bead** **7** and thread the needle back up through the crystal and other seeds.

6 Onto the eyepin thread a cone, a bead cap, a round bead, and another bead cap. Make another wrapped loop at the top.

4 Take the needle through the wire loop at the top, and continue the fringe with a different type of seed bead. Make six fringe strands in this fashion, adding a sparkling crystal at a different place in the sequence each time.

7 To attach the fish hooks, twist the loop open, just like a **jump ring** **5** then thread on the wrapped loop and twist it back to close.

# Beaded Belt

Rabbits are considered bearers of good fortune in many cultures – when I see them happily leaping around the fields on a spring morning I certainly feel fortunate. Jade is also considered to be auspicious by the Chinese and Aztec civilisations, so this belt just has to be lucky. Beaded belts are simple to create because they are really just a longer necklace design. They are obviously quite fragile, so be careful in your choice of extra-strong thread for stringing. When you attach the clasp, make sure it's really secure.

## You will need

2.5cm (1in.) jade rabbit

Oblong cinnabar bead

Triangular cinnabar bead

Gold luck charm

Two gold hearts

Two cinnabar rose beads

Six gold cloisonné beads

Four red cloisonné beads

40 x 4mm red fire-polished beads (FP)

15g (½oz) size 10 red seed beads

Five 8mm crystals

Two necklace ends

Lobster clasp and jump ring

No-stretch nylon bead thread

Flat-nosed pliers

Round-nosed pliers

Wire cutters

Scissors

Needle

Glue

**1** Cut a 1.7m (66in.) length of bead thread, and on one end thread on a wire beading needle. On the other end tie several **knots** **6** one on top of each other until they won't pull through a necklace end. Put a dab of glue on the knot and thread on a calotte.

**2** Thread on 4cm (1½in.) of seed beads then a fire-polished, crystal, FP, then another 4cm (1½in.) of seeds, FP, red cloisonné, FP, seeds, FP, gold cloisonné, FP, seeds, crystal, seeds, FP, red cloisonné, FP, seeds, FP, gold cloisonné, FP, seeds, FP, heart, FP, seeds, FP, oblong cinnabar, FP, seeds, and FP.

**4** Retrace the path of the original thread back up through all the beads as far as the last gold cloisonné bead. Thread on a fire-polished, and continue threading symmetrically as for the first side. When you get to the top, continue the pattern sequence, adding in the two remaining cloisonné beads. This will ensure that the rabbit tassel dangles to one side, even though the clasp is at the back.

**3** Thread on a gold cloisonné, fire-polished, crystal, rabbit bead, FP, oblong cinnabar, FP, 2.5cm (1in.) seeds, triangular cinnabar, FP, 1cm (½in.) seeds, and the charm. Now thread the needle back up through the last FP, creating a loop so the charm hangs free.

**5** Thread on a **necklace end** **1** and knot as before. Close the necklace end, and add a clasp on one side and a **jump ring** **5** on the other, closing the necklace end with round-nosed pliers.

# Marcasite Watchband

I have endeavored to keep the spirit of the Art Deco age alive in this glittering piece. Platinum set with diamonds was the most sought after combination for the wealthy flapper, but as I don't have the wallet of the Rockefellers, this one is mainly marcasite and shiny black onyx, with crystals, pearls, and gold-leaf beads for extra decadence.

## You will need

Watch face

A four-hole clasp

Four 5mm black onyx round beads

Two 2.5cm (1in.) flat art beads

15g (½oz) of size 7 seeds

16 x 4mm gold crystals and

16 x 4mm silver crystals

12 x 4mm hematite crystals

Eight black rice pearls

Four lengths of 35cm (14in.) 0.015mm plastic-coated metal wire

Eight tubular crimps

Flat-nosed pliers

Round-nosed pliers

Wire cutters

**1** Take two strands of plastic-coated metal wire, and thread them both through the loop on one side of the watch face. Thread on a hematite crystal on each side, passing onto both of the threads.

**5** On each double set of wires, thread a hematite crystal, a seed, a silver crystal, and a seed. Cross both sets of thread through a 5mm round bead as shown in step 4.

**2** Choose a wire from each side of the watch face and thread on a seed bead, a silver crystal, and a seed on each. Pass both these threads through the art bead. Thread on a seed, a silver crystal, and a seed on each thread as before.

**3** Take the two other wires and thread on a seed, a pearl, a seed, a gold crystal, a seed, a silver crystal, a seed, a gold crystal, a seed, a pearl, and a seed. Pass the two left-hand threads through a hematite crystal, and then pass the right-hand threads through.

**6** Choose one strand from the left and one from the right. Thread on a seed, a gold crystal, a tubular crimp, and a seed on each. Then thread these wires into the central holes. Pass the wire back down through the beads, and **crush the crimp** **1** with flat-nosed pliers. Trim the wire ends.

**4** Cross both sets of thread through a 5mm bead passing the right-hand threads to the left and the left-hand threads to the right

**7** On the two remaining strands thread a seed, a crystal, a seed, a crimp, and a seed, and pass the right wire through the right hole of the clasp, and the left wire through the left hole then back down through the beads, and crush the crimp. Trim the wire ends. Repeat from the beginning to create the other side.

# Starry Faux Lariat

The owner of my favourite bead store is obsessed with stars. Every time I go in, there's a new star bead she's found and is intent on showing me. So, with a little pile of shooting stars beside me, I threaded more and more onto different strands, and suddenly there was a starry necklace. But the stars didn't seem to shoot, just hang, so I added a couple of long strands that could be tied to let the stars speed downward. This style of necklace – a long strand of beads that is knotted casually at the front – is called a lariat. This one is a fake because it has a clasp at the back.

## You will need

Diamanté ball clasp

Two three-to-one necklace findings

Six silver necklace ends

16 silver crimps

0.5mm nylon beading wire in lengths of 2 x 50cm (20in.),
    1 x 41, 42, 43, 44, 45 and 60cm (16, 16½, 17, 17½,
    18 and 24in.)

Two crystal stars

15g (½oz) of silver seeds

10g (¼oz) of blue Delicas

Five blue and diamanté round beads

Three white frosted stars

Three blue frosted stars

Four iridescent stars

21 x 5mm crystals

Five 4mm blue crystals

12 4mm silver crystals

10 tiny silver stars

11 small silver stars

Flat-nosed pliers

Round-nosed pliers

Wire cutters

**1** Thread the three shortest lengths of wire through a necklace end, and secure with a **crimp** **1** . Repeat for the 44cm (17½in.) and the 45cm (18in.) wires. Combine one 50cm (20in.) length with one 24in.) length; secure with crimp. Repeat with the other 50cm (20in.) and 60cm (24in.) lengths.

**3** Stop threading about 2.5cm (1in.) from the end of the wire; place a crimp on the very end of the wire, and crush. This is just to hold the beads on the wire while you thread up the others.

**2** Start threading silver seed beads on the shortest length first – include one of the iridescent stars and a few tiny and small stars randomly spaced with seeds all the way down the length.

**4** Thread the next wire with blue Delicas, and include a round bead and a few crystals. The third strand is silver with two iridescent stars and a few crystals. The fourth strand is silver and includes a frosted star, crystals, and small silver stars. The fifth is blue with a blue frosted star, a blue round bead, and a few little stars and crystals. Place a crimp on the end of each strand, 2.5cm (1in.) from the end.

**5** Thread the remaining long four strands with one blue and one silver strand on each piece. Use all the remaining small stars and crystals, making the lengths of seeds between large beads less and less. When you reach about 2.5cm (1in.) from the bottom of the silver strand, thread two seeds, a tubular crimp, and two seeds, then a crystal star and two seeds. Thread the end of the nylon wire up through the crimp and a few seeds. Pull tight, and crush the crimp. Trim the nylon wire.

**7** Attach the three-to-one findings to both sides of the clasp, and then attach the necklace ends to the finding, including the five short lengths and one of the long two-strand components.

**6** On the blue strands finish with a frosted blue star, a Delica, and a crystal. Thread on a tubular crimp and crush.

**8** Gather the crimped ends of the three shortest strands, and very carefully snip off the crimp. Thread them through a necklace end, and re-crimp. Close the necklace end around them, and attach to the second three-to-one component. Repeat for the next two lengths, and attach the other long length.

# Wire Work

Wire work is a very ancient art, indeed. In modern times, some enterprising designers have used wire for amazing knitting and crochet projects that include beads within the forms created. Just like beads, wire comes in so many different metals and beautiful colours; I just have to have a skein in every colour and thickness.

# Vintage-Style Chandelier Earrings

This antique type of finding can be very useful for all sorts of projects. Although the findings have a Victorian style, I think that these long earrings have a baroque, almost gypsy look to them. Their rich medieval colours suit the dark wire work admirably, and I love the deep red and purple together as it just looks so regal. Why not incorporate your birth stones with a choice of crystals or add beads to match your new colours. You could even try some coloured wire for a brighter and more contemporary style.

## You will need

Two three-to-one vintage-style necklace ends

Two black fish hooks

Six black headpins

12 x 5cm (2in.) lengths of 4mm black wire

Six 6mm crystals

Six 4mm crystals

Six tumble chips

Six 4mm fire-polished beads

Two 6mm pearls

24 x size 9 seed beads

10 x size 6 seed beads

Flat-nosed pliers

Round-nosed pliers

Wire cutters

**1** Thread a size 9 seed, 4mm crystal, tumble chip, and a size 9 seed onto a headpin, and make a smart top loop. Make a **wrapped loop** 4 .

**2** On one 5cm (2in.) piece of wire, create a small loop about 2cm (¾in.) from the end. Thread this through the previous wrapped loop, and wrap the new loop.

**3** Next thread on a size 6 seed bead, a 6mm crystal, and a size 9 seed. Then make a top loop, and wrap neatly.

**4** On another of the 5cm (2in.) pieces of wire, create a loop about 2cm (¾in.) from the end. Thread this wire through the previous loop, and wrap. Thread on a 9 seed, fire-polished, 9 seed, pearl, and 9 seed. Make a top loop, put this loop through centre of finding; wrap.

**5** Then make the two sets of side pieces, placing the beads in this threading order:
• Bottom section: 6 seed, fire-polished, 9 seed.
• Middle section: 4mm crystal, tumble, 9 seed.
• Top section: 6 seed, 6mm crystal, 9 seed.
Attach these pieces on either side of the finding, using a loop and wrap as before. To attach the finding to the fish hook, twist open the loop, as you would a **jump ring** 5 and thread on the finding, twisting the loop to close.

# Beaded Hoop Earrings

I have several friends who are well-known for their fabulous, and usually huge, earrings. No matter what the occasion, they always seem to have a new and ever more exciting pair. So, not to be outdone, I created this opulent design that combines the always-popular hoop shape with long dangles for maximum effect. The colours within the cloisonné beads dictated the array of crystals and semiprecious chips, giving the final objects an overwhelming look of old Imperial Chinese textiles and embroideries.

## You will need

Four round cloisonné beads

Two long oval cloisonné beads

Eight size 7 gold seeds

20 x 4mm turquoise crystals

Four 3mm magenta crystals

Eight 5mm rose crystals

12 x 5mm green crystals

Four 4mm pink crystals

Eight citrine tumble chips

Four peridot tumble chips

Four 4mm lapis beads

Two 4mm jump rings

Two fish hooks

Two coils of small bracelet memory wire

Six headpins

Memory-wire cutters

Flat-nosed pliers

Round-nosed pliers

Wire cutters

**1** Grip the very end of one piece of memory wire with a pair of round-nosed pliers, and curve it outward. It will be very stiff, but try and make a complete tiny round loop, with no gap. Place it to one side.

**2** Then thread a crystal, cloisonné bead, and a crystal on each of the headpins, using eight turquoise and four green crystals. Make a neat top loop.

**3** Thread on the rest of the beads to the memory wire loop in this order: turquoise, citrine, rose, magenta, rose, citrine, turquoise, green, gold, green, turquoise, and peridot. Then thread on a headpin with one of the round bead dangles.

**4** Thread on a lapis, gold, pink, and the central oval headpin dangle. Repeat the bead threading symmetrically on the other side. Leave 1cm (½in.) of wire showing. Snip off any excess, and then make another loop with the round-nosed pliers.

**5** Open a **jump ring** 5 and thread through the loops from each side of the memory wire. To finish it off, thread on a fish hook, and twist the jump ring to close. Make a second hoop in the same way for the other ear.

# Night Sky Memory-Wire Bracelet

For those of us who like chunky jewellery, this cuff looks as though it has been made from meteorites and pieces of twinkling night sky. I think the overall effect is definitely out of this world! I love the combinations of big faceted stones, but the natural mineral of pyrite has a high amount of copper in it and so it should never be wet or it goes green. Blue goldstone is not a stone at all but is created from glass and sparkling dust. To keep it clean, just polish carefully with a soft dry cloth.

## You will need

Four large three-hole gold spacers
Six 6mm faceted blue goldstone
15cm (6in.) string of blue goldstone tumble chips
12 faceted chunks of pyrite
Three coils of large bracelet memory wire
Six memory-wire ends
15g (½oz) of gold size 6 beads
Epoxy glue
Tape
Memory-wire cutters

**1** Glue three of the memory ends to one end of each wire, using the mixed epoxy glue and a toothpick to apply. Don't worry if you get a tiny bulb of glue at the foot of the bead; it will dry clear. Leave it to dry according to the manufacturer's instructions.

**2** When the glue is completely set, thread on a gold bead, a spacer, and a gold bead. Then thread on two tumble chips, a pyrite piece, a chip, another gold bead, and a second spacer.

**4** Repeat steps 2 and 3 for the second and third wires, threading them through the middle and bottom holes in the spacers. Make sure the length of stones between each spacer is exactly the same as the first – you may have to add or subtract beads because they are all irregular shapes and sizes.

**3** Thread on about 6.5cm (2½in.) of assorted chips and beads, placing a gold bead either side of the 6mm faceted stones. Thread on a gold bead, a spacer, and a gold bead. Wrap a bit of tape on the end of the wire to hold the beads in place until the final cap can be glued on.

**5** Snip off any excess memory wire with the appropriate cutters, leaving 3mm (⅛in.) to glue into a memory-wire end. Be careful: you don't want all the beads to fall off. Glue the remaining three ends to the ends of each wire using the mixed epoxy glue and a toothpick. Leave to dry thoroughly.

# Scarab Choker

Whitby jet was the pinnacle of chic in Victorian times and occasionally you can find fabulous jet beads in antique shops. They sparkle exquisitely from hundreds of hand-cut facets and are just as strong as the day they were made. However, the threads holding them together sometimes disintegrate. This choker is made with all modern beads, but I feel it could very easily have been worn by Mina Harker as she pursued Dracula along the cliff tops at Whitby. Egyptian artefacts were favourite exotic motifs in Victorian times, but this necklace would look just as lovely with a different art-bead centrepiece.

## You will need

Scarab bead

10 x 6mm black onyx beads

28 x 6mm matte black pearls

24 x 4mm jet crystals

14 x 6mm jet crystals

10g (¼oz) of small jet bugle beads

Black nylon bead wire

11 x 5cm (2in.) lengths of 4mm black wire

Two necklace ends and two crimps

Flat-nosed pliers

Round-nosed pliers

Wire cutters

Scissors and glue

**1** Make a small **wrapped loop** `4` on one of the 5cm (2in.) pieces of wire. Thread on the scarab bead, and wrap and trim the other end. Repeat for all 10 of the black onyx beads to make the wire bead components.

**3** Cut an 18cm (7in.) length of nylon wire, and starting at the top of the scarab, thread on the other end of the onyx component, then a 4mm crystal, a small bugle bead, a 6mm crystal, bugle, 4mm, onyx component end, 4mm, two bugles, 4mm, onyx, 4mm, two bugles, 6mm, two bugles, 4mm, onyx, and repeat symmetrically all around the inner circle. Tie the nylon wire in a surgeon's knot and put a dot of glue on the knot. Trim.

**2** Take a 12.5cm (5in.) length of nylon wire, and thread on one end of the scarab, a black onyx component, a 6mm crystal, onyx, 6mm matte bead, onyx, crystal, onyx, matte, onyx, crystal, onyx, other end of the scarab, crystal, and so on, repeating the pattern symmetrically. Tie the nylon wire in a **surgeon's knot** `6` and put a dot of glue on the knot. Trim.

**4** Cut two 50cm (20in.) lengths of nylon wire, and thread one around the outer circumference of beads through each one, along the side of the scarab. Pass one thread from the second onyx component to the fifth; thread another between the third and fourth.

**5** Thread on 5cm (2in.) of bugle beads to the outer two side threads and about 4.5cm (1¾in.) onto the inner thread. Adjust the numbers of beads until all four threads lie flat when joined to enter a 6mm crystal. Thread through all four wires a matte bead, 4mm crystal, a matte bead, 4mm crystal, and 10 matte beads.

**6** Thread on a necklace end and a crimp, and **crush the crimp** **1** with flat-nosed pliers. Trim the wires and close the **necklace end** **1** . Attach one end of a clasp with round-nosed pliers, and repeat from step 4 on the other side.

# Vintage-Style Rose Necklace

This gorgeous cluster of roses is made from oven-baked clay, so if you're feeling creative why not make your own? The rosebuds are fashioned from thin clay strips rolled up between the fingers, baked, then inserted into a sphere of soft clay and baked again.

## You will need

One large rose-inspired bead

Three black headpins

33 x black eyepins

One black lobster clasp

Seven black jump rings

One 4mm gold pearl

10 x 5mm gold pearls

Six 6mm gold pearls

Two 4mm silver pearls

Six 5mm silver pearls

Three 6mm silver pearls

Three 4mm cream pearls

One 5mm cream pearls

Two 6mm cream pearls

Three 4mm mother of pearl (MOP)

10 x 5mm mother of pearl (MOP)

10 x 4mm crystals

Five opal pellets

One teardrop crystal

Two frosted, iridescent, red, size 5 seed beads

Flat-nosed pliers

Round-nosed pliers

Wire cutters

**1** Thread the three headpins with the beads in the following sequences, and create a **small loop** **3** at the top with the round-nosed pliers.

- 4mm MOP, red seed, opal pellet, 4mm cream pearl, 5mm gold pearl.
- 5mm MOP, 5mm cream pearl, crystal, 4mm gold pearl, crystal, opal pellet, 4mm silver pearl.
- Teardrop, 5mm gold pearl, 4mm silver pearl, crystal.

**2** Thread a 6mm cream pearl either side of the rose bead onto an eyepin, and create a loop at the top.

**3** On a second eyepin thread a 4mm cream pearl, a red seed, and another 4mm pearl. Finish by making a loop. Twist one loop to open, and attach the rose component to one end and the three headpins to the other.

**4** For the central triangle, make up these components on eyepins in the same manner as step 3.
- Two crystals, 5mm gold pearl, 5mm MOP, 5mm gold pearl, crystal.
- Two opal pellets, 6mm silver pearl, opal pellet.
- Two crystals, 6mm silver pearl, crystal.
- One 6mm gold pearl, 4mm MOP, 6mm silver pearl, 4mm MOP, 6mm gold pearl.

Attach them together with the **jump rings** **5** or by twisting the eyepins together.

**5** For the final chain, make up all these pieces on eyepins, making sure the loops are all the same size:
- Eight 5mm MOP
- Four 6mm gold pearls
- Six 5mm gold pearls
- Six 5mm silver pearls

Attach them together as before and add to the rest of the necklace. Finally, attach the clasp and a jump ring to the last mother of pearl eyepins by carefully twisting one jump ring open, adding the clasp and top end of necklace, and twisting back to shut. On the other side just add the jump ring. Attach the big rose to the bottom of the central triangle.

# Leaf-and-Chain Earrings

Just before the leaves fall from the trees in Autumn, they seem to hang from the branches by no more than a thread, falling with the slightest breeze. I wanted to re-create that feeling of movement and fragility with these gorgeous iridescent beads and crystals. Because these leaves hang from a fine chain, they move in a more fluid way than ordinary headpin dangles and are light to wear.

## You will need

Six iridescent glass leaves

Six 4mm crystals

Six seed pearls

5cm (2in.) of large trace chain

Six 5cm (2in.) of 0.4mm silver wire

Two silver fish hooks

Flat-nosed pliers

Round-nosed pliers

Wire cutters

**1** Cut the chain into two lengths with eight complete loops in each length. Discard any extra chain. Place the two lengths to one side.

**2** On one 5cm (2in.) piece of wire, create a right angle bend about 1cm (½in.) from the end, using the flat-nosed pliers.

**5** Thread the loop onto the bottom link of the chain, and wrap the loop very neatly.

**3** Thread on a glass leaf with the iridescent side facing the right-angle bend. Bend the wire gently behind the leaf with your fingers to cross just above the bead in a neat triangle. Snip off the excess with wire cutters, and slightly bend the long edge to lie straight upwards using the flat-nosed pliers.

**4** Thread on a crystal and a pearl and create a tiny **loop** **4** 3mm (⅛in.) from the top of the pearl.

**6** Repeat from step 2, adding each dangle from alternate links of chain until you have three leafy dangles. Finally, attach the fish hook by attaching it to the top link of the chain.

# Feather Chandelier Earrings

One of my favourite trims is the huge feather hems seen on those amazing ballroom dancing dresses. I've always nurtured a secret passion for one, and Fred Astaire as a dance partner, of course! Delicate and yet dramatic, these dressy earrings combine freshwater pearls with ostrich feather drops and delicate wire work. Ostrich feather trim is usually sold by the inch or yard, although you can take a few strands from the bottom of a large plume if you prefer. The wired-flower technique could also be used to create a charming necklace, using the earring and feather drop as a central pendant.

## You will need

16 freshwater pearls

16 x 4mm fire-polished beads

Six 4mm jump rings

Two fish hooks

Two cord/feather ends

Two 7.5cm (3in.) of 0.4mm silver wire

Two 20cm (8in.) of 0.4mm silver wire

About 14 strands of ostrich feather

Flat-nosed pliers

Round-nosed pliers

Wire cutters

Glue

**1** Group seven strands of feather in one hand, and trim the top edges to neaten. Put a dab of glue inside the cord end, and push the feathers into it. Crush the cord end tightly around the feathers with flat-nosed pliers. Open and attach a **jump ring** 5 to the top of the cord end.

**3** Make a wrapped loop at the end of an 20cm (8in.) piece of wire, thread on four pearls, curve around to create a loop, and wrap twice around the wrapped loop.

**4** Thread on a fire-polished bead, and pass the wire through the pearl loop. Make a wrapped loop between pearls two and three.

**2** Make a **wrapped loop** 4 with a short piece of wire. Thread on two fire-polished, the feather component, and two fire-polished, and make another wrapped loop. Slightly curve this piece.

**5** Turn over the pearl circle, and thread on another fire-polished bead to the back. Wrap around the loop once more. Thread on four more pearls; make a circle and wrap at the top; then repeat the steps from step 4. Attach the long feather piece to each side of the pearl flowers with 4mm jump rings and attach the fish hook at the top.

# Crystal Heart and Pearl Necklace

I love the sea, and I find myself instantly drawn to things that originated within the ocean's depths. If a country can have a national stone, then New Zealand's is the paua shell. It is the only place where paua, with its shining opalescent colours, is found. It comes from the shellfish of the abalone family and is gathered from the storm-swept beaches of the South Island. The pieces of iridescent shell are then cut and shaped into lovely shapes including stars, dolphins, and hearts. This pretty lightweight necklace could be worn by a mermaid or a surfer girl to remind you always of the ocean.

## You will need

1¾ coils of memory wire

Two memory-wire ends

Seven 5cm (2in.) lengths of 0.4 wire

Two headpins

Three 1cm (½in.) heart beads

Three crystal hearts

One 8mm crystal

Five 5mm crystals

Three 4mm crystals

Four 5mm pearls

120 4mm pearls

Two 6mm pearls

Memory-wire cutters

Glue

Flat-nosed pliers

Round-nosed pliers

Wire cutters

**3** Hold the triangle with one pair of pliers, and with another, wrap the shorter end around the longer twice. Trim close to the stem.

**1** Glue the end onto the memory wire with an epoxy glue; leave it to set until completely solid.

**4** Thread on a 5mm pearl; make a top loop; and make a **wrapped loop** **4** .

**2** To create the centre dangle, make a sharp bend in the wire with the flat-nosed pliers, leaving one 2cm (¾in.) end. Thread the crystal heart on the long end, and very gently make another bend with the pliers to create a U-shape. With your fingers, bend the long end forward to cross the other wire. If you are too heavy handed you will crack the crystal, so be careful.

**5** With another piece of wire, make a loop; thread through the previous loop; wrap; and add a 4mm crystal, a bead heart, and a 5mm crystal.

**6** Make a loop, and wrap at the top of this second component. Add the top component in same way but using a 4mm pearl, an 8mm crystal, and a 4mm pearl. Finish with a top loop, and wrap.

**8** Thread a bead heart, 4mm pearl, 4mm crystal, 4mm pearl, and 5mm pearl on each headpin, and make a wrapped loop at the top.

**7** Create the dangles on both sides in the same manner, but use only two components – the bottom one has a crystal heart and a 5mm pearl, and the upper has a 5mm crystal, 4mm pearl, 6mm pearl, 4mm pearl, and 5mm crystal.

**9** To actually create the necklace, thread on: 54 pearls, a headpin dangle, three pearls, a two-part dangle, three pearls, the centre dangle, and then repeat the pattern symmetrically on the other side. Snip off any extra memory wire, but leave 5mm (¼in.) to glue the other end piece in place.

# Dragonfly Pin

Along the river bank I often see the enormous fairy-like wings of the dragonflies darting around. Their wings' opalescent transparency can be mimicked easily in glass, as Art Nouveau artist René Lalique knew. His dragonflies were legendary, combining the mythology of the dragon in stylized bodies and enormous eyes defined in gold or silver with the delicate iridescent wings copied in glass or enamels. Other artists of the period also used dragonfly and butterfly imagery extensively, including Tiffany in his beautiful stained-glass work. The look is re-created here with the use of attractive coloured beads.

## You will need

2.7m (3yd) of 0.3mm wire

50cm (20in.) of 0.6mm wire

10g (¼oz) of seed beads

Six bugle beads

One 6mm faceted bead

Two size 7 seeds

Stick pin

Epoxy glue

Flat-nosed pliers

Round-nosed pliers

Wire cutters

**1** Cut 15cm (6in.) of 0.3mm wire, and thread the two size 7 beads. Thread one end of the wire back through the beads, creating a loop and pull tight.

**2** Thread the wire ends through the faceted bead, and then thread the six bugle beads.

**3** Thread a seed bead on one wire, and pass the other wire through the bead the other way. Hold the wires in one hand, and twist the two ends together. Trim to 2.5cm (1in.) in length, and slightly curl this end with round-nosed pliers.

**4** With the 0.6mm wire, create a loop about 5cm (2in.) in length. Twist the ends, and make another loop on the other side. Wrap the wire around itself in the centre, and make two more loops. Trim off any excess wire.

**5** Place the body over the wing shape, and secure it by wrapping tightly just below the faceted bead with 0.3mm wire.

**6** Cut a 50cm (20in.) length of 0.3mm wire, and secure it by wrapping around the wing case close to the body. Thread on two beads, and wrap the wire tightly around one wing with the beads pushed to the top and only wire on the underside.

**7** Hold the beads in place, and thread on two more. Continue wrapping seed beads all the way up the wing.

**8** Occasionally wrap the wire around the 0.6mm wire a few times to secure; use different coloured beads to create the wing spots. At the tip of the wing, weave the wire on the back until all the beads are firmly held in place. Trim any excess wire, and repeat for the other three wings.

**9** To make the dragonfly into a pin, glue it to the finding with epoxy glue, and leave it until it is completely set.

# Beaded Flower Hairpins

While looking at some antique couture gowns one day, I noticed one had an adorable corsage of beaded flowers, still sparkling in perfect colours long after the dress had faded. Upon investigation, I discovered this technique is called 'French beading,' and flowers made in this way were a popular type of trimming on hats and gowns in Victorian times. Some examples I have seen are absolutely enormous, about 30cm (1ft) across, and weigh a lot for a hat trim. In contrast to those gargantuan projects, these tiny flowers would look fabulous scattered throughout a swept-up hairstyle. Although very time consuming, in the hands of an experienced artist and using a variety of techniques, just about any flower can be reproduced from seed beads and wire.

## You will need

1.8m (2yd) of 0.4mm wire
15cm (6in.) of 0.3mm green wire
10g (¼oz) of frosted size 10 seeds
10g (¼oz) of colour-lined size 10 seeds
10g (¼oz) of green seeds
Three 4mm yellow crystals
Flat-nosed pliers
Wire cutters

**1** Thread seven frosted seeds onto a 20cm (8in.) length of wire, and twist together a couple of times to secure in a loop.

**2** Thread seven more; twist, leaving a 5mm (¼in.) gap; and repeat until you have four flower petals.

**3** Thread five frosted seeds, four colour seeds, and five frosted seeds, and wrap around the last loop's stem to create the second layer of the petal. Repeat for each of the four petals.

**5** To create the leaves, cut 15cm (6in.) of wire and thread on eleven seeds. Twist to secure for 5mm (¼in.). Add 11 more seeds on one wire, and twist curve into a loop 5mm (¼in.) from the other and twist. Repeat, and then twist wires all the way to the bottom.

**4** Loop the end of the wire back down through the first petal to secure them in a round. Thread on a yellow crystal, and place it in the centre of the petals. Pass the wire over the petals, and wrap till secure. Make two more complete flowers in exactly the same way.

**6** To assemble the bunch, hold all three flowers and the leaf branch and wrap the stalk pieces tightly with wire. Hold against the hairpins, and wrap wire around until secure.

# Looming

Using a loom to weave beads into long strips has its origins in Native American craft traditions. As they did not have written language, these people passed on ideas and messages by pictures and symbolic designs. Many of the designs were originally woven from only two colours of beads and these projects were made from wampum.

# Pre-Raphaelite Bracelet

This bracelet is inspired by some of the background flowers in Pre-Raphaelite artist William Morris's design *The Strawberry Thief.* William Morris was part of the Arts and Crafts movement in the late 19th century. His firm, Morris and Co., strived to provide objects of utility and beauty for the home, designing many beautiful and famous wallpapers and fabrics with which I could quite happily fill my interiors. The company, which originally included artists Edward Burne-Jones and Dante Gabriel Rossetti, was inspired by traditional medieval crafts, such as weaving and embroidery. It often used motifs from nature and heraldry to create its dense, swirling pictorial patterns.

## You will need

10g (¼oz) of each colour of size 11 seeds: light green colour lined, light green iridescent, mid green colour lined, rust colour lined, rust matte, purple/blue colour lined, peach pearlized, red matte iridescent, red colour lined

15g (½oz) of blue matte 11 seeds

18 x 4mm assorted green crystals

Four 4mm gold crystals

Three 4mm red/pink crystals

Perforated clasp finding

0.3mm wire

Strong nylon bead thread

Necklace ends

Sharp needle

Bead loom

Scissors and glue

Flat-nosed and round-nosed pliers

## Pattern chart

Light green colour lined

Light green iridescent

Mid green colour lined

Rust colour lined

Rust matte

Purple/blue colour lined

Peach pearlized

Red matte iridescent

Red colour lined

Blue matte

**1** Thread up the **loom** `8` with 10 strands of thread, and **weave the pattern** `10` according to the chart. If it seems too short, start the pattern again from the beginning and continue until the bracelet is long enough. Don't forget to leave a space for the clasp. Weave the weft ends in neatly **to finish** `9`.

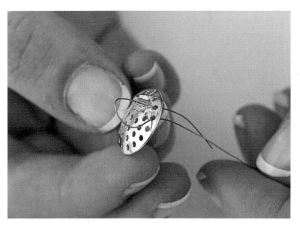

**2** To make the clasp, cut a piece of wire about 25cm (10in.) long and thread one end 2.5cm (1in.) through the clasp. Place a crystal on the wire and thread the wire to the back of the clasp.

**3** Thread the wire to the front of the clasp, and attach another crystal. Continue threading them on the clasp, using green ones around the outside and gold and red ones towards the centre.

**4** To finish, bring the wires to the back of the clasp, twist them together, and trim. Attach the clasp to its back plate by closing the catches with flat-nosed pliers.

**5** Cut the woven piece from the loom, leaving the threads long, and on one side, thread four seed beads to each of the threads. Divide them into two groups, and thread a necklace end to each group.

**6** Tie a knot inside the **necklace end** **1** and put a dab of glue on the knot. Trim the spare thread, and close the necklace end. Repeat for the other group and all threads on the other side. Attach the necklace ends to each piece of the clasp using the round-nosed pliers.

# Loomed Swarovski Bracelet

Looming doesn't have to be only about seed beads. Any beads can be used for weaving on a loom so long as they are all the same size. These crystals come in such a perfect rainbow of colours I couldn't resist creating my own bow of faceted sparkle. This geometric design is quite modern in look but owes its inspiration very much to Art Deco.

## You will need

20 crystals of each colour: rose, fuchsia, ruby, siam, light siam, ocean green, indicolite, emerald, erinite, peridot, light peach, smoky topaz, topaz, peach, light rose, amethyst, lavender, capri blue, sapphire, and light sapphire.

15g (½oz) of size 11 silver seeds

Strong nylon thread

T-bar clasp

Two rondelles

Two necklace ends

Sharp needle

Bead loom

Scissors and glue

Flat-nosed pliers

Round-nosed pliers

## Pattern chart

| | | | |
|---|---|---|---|
| ▢ | Rose | ▢ | Peach |
| ▢ | Fuchsia | ▢ | Light peach |
| ▢ | Ruby | ▢ | Light rose |
| ▢ | Siam | ▢ | Amethyst |
| ▢ | Light siam | ▢ | Lavender |
| ▢ | Ocean green | ▢ | Capri blue |
| ▢ | Indicolite | ▢ | Sapphire |
| ▢ | Emerald | ▢ | Light sapphire |
| ▢ | Erinite | ▢ | Topaz |
| ▢ | Peridot | ▢ | Smokey topaz |

**1** Cut 4m (4½yd) of thread and thread one end onto a needle. **Thread up** **8** the bead loom. As you do so, however, thread 30 silver seeds onto each warp thread, continuing until you have six warp threads. Position the beads within the top weaving area.

**2** Push a seed bead from each thread to the top of the loom, and secure the weft thread below them, on the left-hand thread.

**3** Thread on the crystals from the first row of the pattern chart, and secure by **weaving the needle back** **9** . Push up another row of seed beads, and thread the needle down through the left-hand one.

**5** Remove your work from the loom by cutting the threads carefully, leaving equally long weft threads on each side.

**6** On one side of the work, thread five seeds onto each weft thread, and using a wire needle, thread them all through a rondelle and a necklace end. Tie them securely with a **square knot** **6** and put a dab of glue on the knot.

**4** Continue threading crystals and pushing up rows of seeds, following the pattern chart. When the design is complete, secure the weft thread with a knot and by weaving it back through the work.

**7** Close the **necklace end** **1** with flat-nosed pliers, and fasten on one end of the clasp with the round-nosed pliers. On other side, attach the other part of the clasp.

# Bead Woven Choker

This style of bone choker is almost synonymous with handcrafted jewellery. Originally, different motifs or large beads, quill rosettes, or feathers were placed in the centre of the piece. I decided to use a bead-loomed motif representing two hummingbirds. The hummingbird was representative of both a clever homemaker and a small but spirited fighter in traditional designs. It is usually seen as a double design because the hummingbird is one of a faithful pair. You could even design and weave your own special centrepiece, but if you do, keep it to the same dimensions as mine or the rest of the choker won't work.

## You will need

Six 5cm (2in.) bone tubes

Six 2.5cm (1in.) bone tubes

20 x 6mm round lapis beads

16 x 6mm round crystals

72 cylinder turquoise chips

Two large three/five hole spacers

Six silver necklace ends

10g (¼oz) of size 11 seeds in cream, cobalt, pearl
    turquoise, kingfisher blue, dark frosted blue, and
    green

Strong bead thread

T-bar clasp

Bead loom

Sharp needle

Scissors and glue

Wire needles

Round-nosed pliers

## Pattern chart

☐ Cream

■ Cobalt

▧ Pearl turquoise

▨ Green

▨ Kingfisher blue

▨ Dark frosted blue

**1 Set up the loom** 8 with 18 threads, and **weave up** 10 the pattern using the chart as a guide. **Finish off** 9 the threads carefully and neatly.

**2** Next, cut the threads on the underside of the loom so that there are equally long lengths on each side of the woven piece.

**3** Place the woven piece flat in front of you, and thread a wire needle with the top right three threads; thread on a turquoise cylinder, a crystal, and another cylinder. Thread the next three threads with a second wire needle, and repeat.

**4** Then thread both needles through one of the 5cm (2in.) bone beads. On the top needle, thread on a cylinder, a lapis bead, and a cylinder. Pass it through the top hole of the spacer; thread on a cylinder, a lapis bead, and another cylinder. Repeat with the second needle.

**5** Pass both needles through a 2.5cm (1in.) bone pipe and then through a necklace end. Tie the two groups of threads together with a square knot. Put a dab of glue on the knot; trim; and close the necklace end.

**6** Repeat from step 3 for the all threads, but reverse the lapis and crystal beads.

**7** Attach the **necklace ends** 1 to the clasp using round-nosed pliers.

# Embroidery

Beaded gowns and accessories have always been popular but were once only available to the very wealthy. We are fortunate to live in an age when machines are the predominant source of commercial embroidery. Less than a hundred years ago, all embroidery including beads, sequins, and gold threads had to be applied by hand.

# Fringed Bag

I love fringes, they have a life of their own, dancing and shimmying all by themselves. This wonderful fringe is called coral or branching fringe and creates a dense texture very quickly. I was given the lovely coral chips as a gift after a friend went on an expedition to a gem store and remembered my penchant for pink! A ready-made small bag is the basis for this project, so either embellish one you already have or buy a cheap one especially for the project. I made this one from the remnants of a 1920s-style dress made by another friend.

## You will need

Vintage fabric bag approx. 10 x 15cm (4 x 6in.)

10g (¼oz) of coral Delicas

10g (¼oz) of colour-lined coral size 11 seeds

10g (¼oz) of pearlized coral size 11 seeds

10g (¼oz) of peach size 10 seeds

5cm (2in.) string of angel coral chips

Fine beading thread

Sharp needle

Scissors

**1** Thread up a needle with 90cm (1yd) of thread and make a **couple of stitches** 12 at one bottom corner edge of bag to secure. Thread on about 12 size 10 seeds. Use the bottom bead as a turning bead, and pass the needle up through five beads. 16

**2** Thread on around 12 more seeds. Once more use the bottom bead as a turning bead, and pass the needle up through five beads. Make a final branch in the same way.

**3** On the final branch, pass the needle all the way up to the top of the stem, bypassing the branches, and pull until firm but not too tight or it will not hang correctly. Make a stitch at the top to secure; then move on to another spot 1cm (½in.) away, passing the needle along the inside of the bag.

**4** Make another stitch to secure, and make a second dangle. Continue all the way along the bottom of the bag, varying the length and quantity of the branches. Finish off the thread at the end. Repeat from step 1 with the pearl coral beads along the bag, too.

**5** For the second row of the fringe, continue creating branches in exactly the same way about 1cm (½in.) above the first row, but use the Delicas and the colour-lined beads. Be careful not to sew through to the back of the bag. I usually keep my hand inside it to prevent any accidents.

**6** To create the coral clumps, thread on about four coral twigs and make a stitch to secure before moving to the next position. Thread on extra beads to the ribbon tie for added decoration if you like.

# Cut-Velvet Scarf

This is an amazing fabric base for beading. Although beautiful in its own right, it also lends itself to embroidery as you have a pattern already there that you can enhance, using assorted small beads to greater effect. Cut-velvet is created when different threads are used to weave the pile and the supporting fabric. The pattern is screen printed using a chemical that dissolves the pile threads in the areas it contacts, leaving the background fabric as a contrasting texture, just like magic. This is a freeform project, so add as many or as few beads as you like. I suggest using beads the same colour as the pile sections, but you could go for a complete contrast as well.

## You will need

Cut-velvet scarf

15g (½oz) of matte seed beads size 11

15g (½oz) of shiny seed beads size 11

15g (½oz) of Japanese bugle beads

Fine beading thread

Sharp needle

Scissors

**1** Look at the scarf and decide what motifs will be best enhanced by bead work – choose large distinct areas such as big flowers. I concentrated my embroidery on the bottom half to give weight to the scarf and help it hang nicely. Thread up a needle with 90cm (1yd) of fine beading thread and make a couple of **little stitches** **12** to secure.

**4** To create the seed bursts in the centre of the flowers, **couch** **14** alternate lengths of seven and four seed beads in a star burst pattern.

**2** To create the angled bugle outlines, which are best used for thick stems and leaves, thread on a bugle, and pass the needle back so that it emerges from the fabric, halfway down the bead.

**5** To create the beaded buds, thread on three seed beads. Pass the needle down through the fabric to emerge at right angles from the row of beads.

**6** Thread a seed; then pass the needle through the centre bead of the three. Add on another seed, maintaining the straight line, pass the needle down through the fabric once more.

**3** Thread on another bugle, and place it so that it lies parallel to the first. Pass the needle down and up through the fabric again, halfway down the second bugle, and repeat as necessary.

**7** Continue embellishing until you are happy. It is better to embellish fewer motifs in a denser way than to spread too thinly over a large area. **Secure the thread** **13** firmly by making a few tiny stitches in an inconspicuous place.

# Bead Weaving

In the same way that knitting and crochet have a repertoire of stitches so does beading. Unlike traditional weaving no loom is required, just a needle and thread, which loop and attach one small bead to another in a wide variety of techniques. New stitches are discovered all the time, as well as old favourites learned from generations of traditional work passed down through families of beaders.

# Spiral Rope Bracelet

This bracelet was for my mother-in-law, Jacqui, in her favourite golden colours. She belongs to a bewildering assortment of societies and often goes out to lunch meetings and smart evening dinner parties. I created this for her as an icebreaker, not that she needs one! But you can't really miss such a fabulous bracelet and once spotted it has to be commented on. The spiral rope is so easy to stitch, all the impressive size grading comes from simply using bigger beads in the centre section.

## You will need

T-bar clasp

15g (½oz) of bronze size 9 seed beads

15g (½oz) of gold size 10 seed beads

60 small gold beads (size 6)

40 x 4mm transparent gold crystals

10 x 4mm gold pearls

Fine or strong nylon thread

Fine sharp beading needle

Scissors

**1** Cut and thread up a 1.4m (1½yd) length of nylon thread. Thread a firm **stopper bead** `7` leaving a tail of 15cm (6in.). Thread five gold and six bronze seeds. To start the **spiral rope** `18` pass the needle up through the five gold seeds.

**3** For the next section, thread on a gold seed, two bronze seeds, a small gold bead, and two bronze seeds. Pass the needle up through the top five gold seed beads as before. Work spiral stitch with this sequence for 10 rows.

**2** Thread a gold seed and six bronze seeds, and work a **spiral rope** `18` stitch with one gold and six bronze seeds, for 20 rows, passing the needle always through the top five gold beads.

**4** The next threading sequence is a gold seed, bronze seed, gold bead, crystal, gold bead, and a bronze seed. Pass the needle up through the top five gold seeds as before. Work spiral stitch with this sequence for 10 rows.

**5** The centre section has no gold bead or bronze seeds – it is simply a gold seed, crystal, 4mm pearl, and crystal. Work spiral stitch with this sequence for ten rows. If you have to **add thread** [20] do so using a **square knot** [6] and weave the ends in.

**7** Weave the needle around and around, following in the path of the spiral rope stitches to secure the thread. Trim the thread when you feel it is secure. Unthread the stopper bead and add the clasp using this tail on the other side, securing and trimming as before.

**6** Repeat the threading sequence and number of rows from step 4, then step 3, and finally step 2. To add clasp, thread on three bronze seeds, the clasp, and three more seeds. Pass the needle around through the seeds and clasp once more for strength.

# Daisy Chain Anklet

As summer draws near, I look for the little pink edged daisy flowers. I think they are lovely and spent many a happy hour chaining them together as a girl, and was always sad when they wilted. At last I have a solution! This daisy chain will always stay perky. What a great present for a little girl. The pearls are high quality fakes made from crystal; if you use another sort make sure the pearl coating won't chip off.

## You will need

Toggle clasp

Eight 6mm lemon pearls

64 x 4mm cream pearls

20 jade tumble chips

10g (¼oz) of size 10 jade seed beads

1m (40in.) strong nylon thread

Two sharp needles

Scissors

**1** Thread each end of the nylon thread with the needles. On the right needle, thread one side of the clasp and five seed beads. On the left needle, thread five seeds beads and a tumble chip.

**3** Cross the threads by passing one needle from left to right and the other from right to left through a 4mm pearl.

**2** Pass the right-hand needle from right to left through the tumble chip so that the threads cross within it. Thread a tumble chip on each needle.

**4** Add a 4mm pearl on each needle, and cross the threads through a 6mm lemon pearl.

**5** Next thread on a 4mm pearl on each side, and cross through a 4mm pearl. Pass what is now the right-hand needle, clockwise through the next pearl along, and add a 4mm pearl to fill the gap.

**6** Continue passing the needle clockwise around the pearls adding another 4mm in the left-side gap. Cross threads once more through the top pearl.

**7** Thread two seeds, a tumble chip, and two seeds, and repeat the flower sequence from step 3. Continue this flower and leaf sequence until you have eight flowers.

**8** Finally, thread a tumble chip on each needle, and cross through another chip. On the right-hand needle, pick up five seeds, the other side of the clasp, and five more seeds. Pass the needle through the tumble chip, and go up through all the seeds and clasp to reinforce it.

**9** Tie a **square knot** **6** and weave the ends of the thread round the flowers in opposite directions. Trim any remaining thread.

# Buried Bugle-Bead Necklace

This long 1920s-style necklace is punctuated by clusters of exciting beaded shapes, which look fabulous but are actually terribly easy to make. I have constructed three types using the same technique but with different beads each time, to give you an idea of the possibilities. As for the necklace itself, it could be worn flapper style as a long string or wrap it twice around the neck for a shorter but denser bead necklace. You could even use it as a bracelet or bag strap – talk about versatile!

## You will need

15g (½oz) of size 10 green seeds
15g (½oz) of size 10 purple seeds
15g (½oz) of size 10 blue seeds
15g (½oz) of 10mm silver bugles
15g (½oz) of size 7 blue and green seeds
15g (½oz) of 4mm blue fire-polished
15g (½oz) of 4mm green fire-polished
15g (½oz) of 4mm AB crystals
Strong nylon bead thread
Sharp needle
Scissors

**1** Cut 1.9m (2yd) of thread. Thread on a **stopper bead 7** very securely, about 10cm (4in.) from the end.

**2** To create the purple cluster, thread on a blue seed, a bugle, and a blue seed.

**3** Next thread on two purple seeds, a crystal, and two seeds. Pass the needle up through the seed-bugle-seed creating a loop and tighten.

**4** Repeat step 3 four more times; then thread on thirty size 10 green seeds.

**5** To make the green cluster, thread on a purple seed, a bugle, and a purple seed. Next thread on a green size 7 seed, a purple size 10 seed, a green fire polish, a purple seed, and a green seed. Pass the needle up through the seed-bugle-seed, creating a loop, and tighten. Repeat four more times. Thread on 30 size 10 green seeds.

**6** For the blue cluster, thread on a blue size 10 seed, a bugle, and a blue seed. Next, thread on a blue size 10 seed, a blue size 7 seed, a blue fire-polished, a blue size 7 seed, and a blue size 10 seed. Pass the needle up through the seed-bugle-seed creating a loop, and tighten. Repeat four more times. Thread on 30 size 10 green seeds.

**7** Repeat the pattern of purple, green, blue, green, purple, green, blue, green, with thirty seeds in between until the necklace is the right length.

**8** Tie the two ends together with a **square knot** 6 .

# Egyptian-Style Netted Necklace

When I was in Egypt on my honeymoon, I saw the most incredible netted necklaces in the Cairo museum. They were so intricately constructed, it was hard to believe they had been made as early as 2000 B.C. I knew I just had to make one. It took a little while to work out how to stitch the top of the necklace tighter, so it would curve more than the bottom, but the final design of this spectacular necklace is actually very straightforward to construct. It is extremely time-consuming however, so be prepared to bead slowly and carefully, for a couple of hours at a time, over a week or two. The final result is definitely worth being patient.

## You will need

25g (1oz) of size 9 blue seed beads (b9)

30 antique gold size 7 seed beads (ag7)

15g (½oz) of bright gold size 7 seed beads (bg7)

25g (1oz) of antique gold size 5 seed beads (ag5)

15g (½oz) of blue bugles (bb)

25g (1oz) of turquoise bugles (tb)

76 x 4mm lapis lazuli beads (ll4)

75 x 4mm green opal crystals (gc4)

Strong bead thread

Sharp needle

Scissors

**2** Use the bottom bg7 as a turning bead, and thread the needle back up through the 2 x tb, ag5, 2 x b9s, ag7, gc4, and ag7.

**3** Thread on a bb, 3 x b9s, and pass the needle back up through the bg7 already threaded.

**4** Add on 2 x b9s, ag7, tb, ag7, and pass the needle up through the ll4.

**5** Thread an ag7, tb, bg7, 2 x b9s, and pass the needle up through the ag7s.

**6** Add 2 x b9s, ag7, and pass the needle through the very first bead threaded, the b9.

**1** Cut a 2m (a good 2-yd) length of thread. Thread on a firm **stopper bead** 7 and then thread on a b9, ag7, 2 x b9s, ag7, 2 x b9s, bg7, tb, ag7, ll4, ag7, tb, ag7, 2 x b9s, bg7, 3 x b9, bb, ag7, gc4, ag7, 2 x b9s, ag5, 2 x tb, and bg7.

**7** Add 2 x b9s, ag7, and pass the needle down through the top b9 to make a picot edge.

**8** Thread 2 x b9s, ag7, and pass the needle down through the top b9.

**9** Add on a b9, ag7, 2 x b9s, and pass the needle down through the bg7.

**10** Add a tb, ag7, ll4, ag7, tb, and pass the needle down through the ag7.

**11** Thread 2 x b9s, bg7, 2 x b9s, and pass the needle down through the third b9.

**12** Thread on a bb, ag7, gc4, ag7, b9s, ag5, 2 x tb, and a bg9.

**13** Repeat from step 2 until all the lapis and crystal beads have been used. When you have to add thread, tie a **square knot** [6] and leave the ends long to **weave** [21] through the pattern. I usually do them all at the end, but you can neaten as you go along if you prefer.

**14 Finish** `21` your last row with the thread at the top of the necklace. To make the fastenings, thread on 2 x b9 beads, a 4mm lapis bead, and a b9. Using the last bead as a turning bead, turn and thread back through the lapis and two seeds.

**15** Weave round the top circle of seeds, and go up and down through the lapis again to reinforce it. Weave the needle down to the next blue seed section, and attach another 4mm lapis in the same way. Finish off the thread by weaving it very securely back through the work.

**16** On the other side of the necklace, take off the stopper bead, and thread on around 12 seed beads. Make a loop; attaching it up through the seeds you've already woven. Check the bead fits snugly through the loop – this will be your necklace's fastening so make sure it won't slip out. Adjust the number of seeds as necessary. Go around the loop again for strength and weave down to the next blue seed section, attaching another seed loop in the same way. Finish off the thread by weaving it very securely back through the work.

# Netted Bead Choker

This bead is an exotic treasure, a delicious Fabergé egg of Russian-style glamour. After trying this design with seeds I ended up with a bead the size of a golf ball, so I strongly advise keeping with the Delicas. They are so tiny they don't overwhelm the bead. As well as a necklace, it could be used as a key fob or tree decoration, or even as the head of a tassel or a light pull. This is a six bead netting design, which creates a very loose and stretchy net; you could also try a tighter weave of three bead netting for a smaller, less ostentatious bead.

## You will need

2.5cm (1in.) long oval wooden bead

14 x 3mm crystals

10g (¼oz) of size 10 seed beads

10g (¼oz) of Delicas

Nylon thread

1½ coils memory wire, necklace size

Two end caps

Glue

Scissors

Sharp needle

**1** Cut 1.4m (1½yd) of nylon thread, leaving a 7.5cm (3in.) tail, and thread on a **stopper bead** **7**. Thread on: seed bead, five Delicas, seed, five Del., crystal, five Del., crystal, five Del., seed, five Del., seed, five Del., seed, and five Del.

**2** Pass the needle up through the second crystal, creating a loop of beads at the end of the string. Pull the thread tight.

**3** Add five Delicas, a crystal, and five Delicas, and pass the needle through the second seed bead that you threaded.

**4** Add five Delicas, a seed, five Delicas, a seed, and five Delicas. Pass needle down through top crystal.

**5** Add five Delicas, a crystal, and five Delicas, and pass the needle through the bottom-right seed bead.

**6** Add five Delicas, seed, five Delicas, seed, and five Delicas, and repeat from step 2.

**7** Repeat until you have used all the crystals. When the net is in front of you, with the stopper bead at the top left-hand side, your needle should be emerging from the bottom-right seed bead.

**8** To join the net together into a tube, thread five Delicas, seed, and five Delicas, and pass the needle up through the bottom-left seed.

**9** Thread five Delicas, and pass the needle through the last crystal threaded.

**10** Add five Delicas, and pass the needle through the first crystal threaded. Add five more Delicas, and pass needle through the opposite seed bead. Thread five more Delicas, and pass the needle through the first bead threaded.

**11** Add a Delica, and pass the needle through each top seed bead adding a Delica between each. Pull tight and go around the circle again.

**12** Weave the thread down the netting, emerging through a seed bead. Repeat step 11, but before you pull tight, insert the bead. Weave all the ends up and down in the work, and trim when secure.

**13** To create the choker, glue an end on the memory wire with epoxy glue. Thread seed or Delica beads halfway along; add the big bead; and continue to thread seeds. Finish by gluing another end on.

# Hemp Choker

I made this hemp choker for my husband who demanded I design something manly for him to put his wedding ring on when he goes to the gym. I decided to use all his favourite earthy coloured stones within it, echoing the shapes and colours of the natural world, as he's a real outdoors type. Hemp is such a fabulous natural fibre, it's strong and has a great texture but you could also make this necklace from a thin round leather thong – or for a futuristic look how about a rubber cord? Even a fluffy textured knitting yarn could look amazing with big crystals instead of beads.

## You will need

Four 8mm tiger eyes

Four 8mm green aventurines

Four 8mm picture jaspers

Two 8mm goldstone

Two 8mm malachites

One 8mm carnelian

90cm (1yd) of strong bead thread

4.5m (5yd) of hemp yarn

Two leather ends

T-bar clasp

Two 4mm jump rings

Glue

Flat-nosed pliers

Round-nosed pliers

Scissors

**1** Find the centre of the hemp yarn, add the end of the bead thread, and tie an **overhand knot** **6** to secure all three together. I leave the hemp in a loop so that I can attach the ends to a hook or nail, making the knots easier to tie.

**4** Now thread this right-hand hemp up through the loop on the left-hand side. The hemp strands will now have changed sides and the bead thread will be caught through the centre of the knot.

**2** Arrange the threads so you have hemp strand each side of the bead cord. Make the left-hand hemp thread into a small loop and cross it above the bead thread. Hold firmly with your thumb and finger where the two threads cross.

**3** Make a loop with the right-hand hemp thread, crossing over the left-hand hemp thread's tail, then passing under the central bead thread.

**5** Gently pull the knot until it is firm but not tight. Practise a bit until you find the correct tension – just like knitting everyone will knot differently.

**6** Repeat from step 1 until you have 10 knots. It will begin to gently spiral clockwise. Try to keep all the knots the same size and firmness to create a smart uniform piece.

**7** Thread a tiger eye bead onto the central bead thread, and pass the hemp either side to work a knot directly under it, holding the bead in place. Continue knotting another 10 times and add a green aventurine bead. Then continue knotting and threading beads in this sequence: picture jasper, tiger eye, green aventurine, goldstone, malachite, picture jasper, carnelian, picture jasper, malachite, goldstone, green aventurine, tiger eye, picture jasper, green aventurine, and tiger eye.

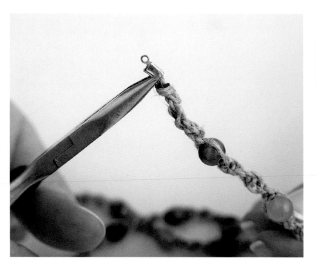

**8** Finish with ten knots of spiral and knot threads together. Remove the rope from hook and trim both ends 5mm (¼in.) from the knot. Put a dab of glue on one end, and place in a leather end. Close the **leather end** 2 around it with flat-nosed pliers. Repeat on other side.

**9** Attach the T-bar clasp with a **jump ring** 5 twisting to open.

# Garnet Cross

In Tudor times, fabulous jewel encrusted crosses were owned by the wealthy English noblemen of the day, proclaiming both their devotion to God and their household riches. As explorers brought back new and exciting gems from their discovered lands, ever more splendid jewellery was designed and presented to royalty. I designed a slightly less ostentatious piece which nevertheless retains a flavour of the courts of Henry VIII and Elizabeth I. The garnet and crystal cross is woven in the Japanese style that, although it looks fabulously intricate, is in fact very simple to create. It uses just one very clever technique: crossing two threads in opposite directions through a bead. Many gorgeous Japanese crystal pendant motifs are created in this way, just using seeds and crystals to produce a huge variety of shapes from hearts to horseshoes.

## You will need

20 x 4mm garnet beads

48 x 4mm crystals

10g (¼oz) of size 10 seed beads

Nylon beading wire, approx. 90cm (1yd)

Strong beading thread

90cm (1yd) strand of tumble chip garnets

Scissors

Glue

**1** Thread on three crystals, and move them down to the centre of the nylon beading wire. You will be working with both ends of the wire at the same time. Take the right-hand thread, and pass it from right to left through a fourth crystal. Take the left-hand thread, and pass it from left to right through the fourth crystal, too, so that the threads cross inside it. Pull the threads tight, creating a circle.

**2** Thread a crystal on each wire, and cross the threads through a seventh crystal. Next thread a crystal on each, and cross wires through a garnet bead. Continue this pattern until you have four garnet beads in sequence.

**3** On the right-hand thread, pick up a garnet, a crystal, a garnet, and three crystals. Pass the thread back through the second garnet, making the three crystals into a loop.

**4** Add on a crystal, and pass the thread through the first crystal to make a second loop. Repeat from step 3 with the left-hand wire to make the second arm of the cross.

**5** Pass the two threads left and right through a garnet bead, and add a crystal on each thread.

**6** Continue the weaving pattern as illustrated, ending with a crystal on each thread.

**7** Cross the wires through the crystal at the end so that the cross is now joined at the top and bottom.

**8** Continue one thread through the next two of these bottom crystals. The threads should now be emerging from equal crystals on opposite sides of the front and back of the cross.

**9** To weave the front and back together, thread each end up through the next woven crystal, and cross them through a seed bead. Thread each up through the next crystal, and then cross through another seed bead.

**10** Continue all the way around the edge of the cross. At the top, pass both threads through one crystal, and continue as before. At the bottom, tie a **square knot** **6** and dab on epoxy glue.

**11** Thread half the garnets onto the strong bead thread and string on the cross through the top crystal. Continue threading all the rest of the garnets, and tie the strands with a square knot. Pass the thread ends back down through the tumble chips to neaten.

# Art Deco Bracelet

Stone doughnuts are traditional shapes for pendants in China and while I love them, I can't often think of enough interesting things to do with them. Then one day, I was looking at Art Deco shapes of jewellery and was suddenly inspired to create a peyote stitch setting for this lovely pink stone ring. The odd count peyote stitch is slightly more complicated than the even count version described in basic techniques. It takes a bit of practice, but it's worth persevering because it's so useful. It's also essential if you want a strip with a symmetrical pattern, as we do for this project.

## You will need

Stone doughnut 3cm (1¼in.) across with 1cm (½in.) hole

Lobster clasp

Strong nylon thread

Two 4mm rondelles

Four 4mm pink pearls

Four 4mm crystals

10g (¼oz) of main colour Delicas

10g (¼oz) of five other colours of Delicas

Long beading needle

Step two

Step three, four, and five

Step nine

**2** Add a tenth Delica and weave the needle from right to left, through the eighth bead. Add a Delica, and pass needle through the sixth Delica. Add one more, and pass the needle through the fourth Delica. Add another, and pass the needle through the second and the first beads.

**3** Thread on a Delica (number 14), and pass the needle up from left to right through the second and third Delicas of the original row.

**4** Pass the needle back down through numbers 13, two, and one.

**1** Using a 1m (3ft) length of strong nylon thread, place a **stopper bead** **7** on the thread about 45cm (1½ft) from the end. You will return to this piece of thread to add the clasp. To begin the **peyote stitch** **19** thread on nine Delicas.

**5** Pass the needle from left to right through the last added bead (number 14). You will now have a ladder and are ready to start the third row.

**6** For the third row, weave a Delica from left to right, through each sticking out bead of the previous row.

**8** Repeat the bead-adding sequence from step 6, using the different coloured Delicas, until you are ready start the decrease.

**7** Weave down from right to left to the last space (bead number 22). Pass the needle through the last two beads (numbers 15 and 14); add a bead; and pass the needle left to right through 14 and 13. Pass the needle down from right to left through 17, 16, and 14, then back from left to right through 15.

**9** To decrease, finish the row so that you have four beads sticking out and the needle emerging from the end bead. Pass the needle from right to left through the last two beads of the previous row, and thread needle back from left to right up through the last bead added.

**10** Continue weaving the thinner row in the same way to the end of the chart. When you finish the last row, be sure to leave the thread end nice and long.

**13** Add five Delicas, and weave your thread down through the bottom Delica, around and around through the work until you are in a position to repeat step 12, reinforcing the clasp. Weave the thread end securely through the work, and trim. Make and attach the other strap in the same fashion, and add other side of the clasp in same way, too.

**11** Wrap the thin end around the doughnut, and attach it like a zipper by weaving the beads together with the long thread end. Secure thread by weaving back zigzag through the work and trim.

**12** On the other end of the strap, unthread the stopper bead and thread on five Delicas, a crystal, Delica, pearl, rondelle, pearl, Delica, crystal, and clasp or jump ring, and then go back down through all the beads to the second crystal.

# Frilled Peyote Bracelet

Who needs diamonds? While I occasionally think it might be nice to own a big diamond bracelet, I have to admit this seeded cuff sparkles like a starlet on Oscar night. Its secret is in the silver-lined seed beads, which when woven in this three-dimensional form seem to sparkle even more than usual. Not being able to help myself, I added a glitzy clasp and yet more crystals – suddenly what might otherwise be a clever but dull bracelet turned into an expensive looking work of art, which friends keep asking to borrow.

## You will need

15g (½oz) of size 10 silver-lined seed beads
Six sew-on crystals
Crystal set clasp, two hole
Four 1cm (½in.) pieces of gimp/French wire
Strong nylon thread
Thread conditioner
Sharp needle
Scissors

**1** Cut 1m (40in.) of nylon thread, and thread on a **stopper bead** `7` about 40cm (15in.) from the end. Thread the needle with the other end, and pick up 80 seed beads.

**2** Pick up another seed bead, and create **peyote stitch** `19` down the length of the row. Work two more rows of peyote up and down. If you run out of thread, add **some more** `20`.

**3** Continue with another row of the stitch, but pick up and add two beads in each gap instead of just one. This will create the frill on one side, so keep the tension tight but expect it to twirl all over the place.

**4** Thread the nylon thread up and down along the top edge of the weave, and work a row of peyote along the non-frilled edge. Then make the frill on this side in the same way as described in step 3. Finish with the thread emerging from one corner.

**5** Thread a piece of gimp and pass it through one end of the clasp. Thread back through a seed bead and work the needle up and down, zigzagging through the seeds until it is totally secure. Repeat for the other corner of the weave and the other hole of the clasp.

**6** Weave the needle down the seeds, and sew on a crystal in the centre of the strip, sewing straight through the seeds. When it's totally secure, weave down 1cm (½in.) passing the needle through the beads and sew on another crystal – repeat for a third sparkle.

**7** Finally attach the other end of the clasp and crystals in exactly the same way, and remember to buy yourself a new evening dress!

# Designing Your Own Jewellery

All designers have their own preferred ways of working – some meticulously draw out a clear plan of their end product, including every component and how it will be joined together, others start with a pile of beads and a picture in their head and see where it goes! No matter how they work, every designer I've met is a secret horder, building up a collection of useful and beautiful beads to draw from, often buying unusual pieces when they see them and deciding exactly how to use them at a later date.

This is not to say that designers randomly buy every bead they see. They will often have a collection of pieces forming in their mind when they go bead shopping, or even a specific type of beaded work that is instantly recognisable as their style. We are often drawn back time and time again to specific colours or shapes, so try to analyse why you like the things you do. Is it because they are dainty, chunky, or spiky? Are you always drawn to flowers or do you always buy blue? Two people given exactly the same set of beads will think of very different ways to use them, reflecting their own tastes and style.

A designer's aim is to cultivate something in their work that makes it instantly recognisable as theirs. While they will often be inspired by other people's ideas, they will take the ball and run with it, often ending up with a product far removed from their original inspiration. It is a good idea to start keeping a scrapbook of images you like, such as pieces of jewellery seen in fashion magazines, colours that look good together; even the shapes of objects completely unrelated to jewellery may spark off a new idea.

I like to carry a small notebook around with me wherever I go, just to doodle in with a cheap pen. Don't worry about the artistic style, no one will ever see your ideas book, and you can always jot down notes in words, as well as pictures, if you don't feel confident with drawing. A good starting point for inspiration is often the past. I like to look at historical pieces in museums and auction catalogues, particularly 1920s and Victorian fashion papers. But you might feel enthused by chunky jade of the Incas or the subtle floral designs of ancient Japan. The Internet is a wonderful resource for designers, just put in a few key words and have a wander. Remember a piece that was originally made by silversmithing can often be reinterpreted in beads.

Another good design tool available from art shops is a colour wheel; this shows colours with their complementary and harmonious hues. A complementary colour is one which we often think of as opposite, orange and blue, purple and yellow, red and green. A harmonious colour is one similar to the main colour, blue and purple, yellow and orange for example. Of course not every shade of blue looks good with every shade of orange – try putting different beads next to each other and group tubes of seed beads in sets that look nice to you. Look for the complementary colours that will provide a zingy contrast as well as those that blend in harmony.

You might like the simplicity of classical Greek patterns or fall for the looping swirls of the Art Nouveau. Keep drawing shapes and thinking about what methods you could use to bring these ideas to life. A simple Greek key pattern could be created for a bracelet on a loom but how will you do it up? You could use a bead and loop, or a smart clasp, or attach it to ribbon and sew hook-and-eye fastening tape to create a seamless band. There are many possibilities and all give a different feel to the work.

Don't attempt too much to begin with – if you start a long and complicated project without a clear idea of how you are going about it or how long it is likely to take, you're likely to get discouraged halfway through and never finish it. Create a few smaller designs to try out your ideas and techniques first. Don't be afraid to go wrong – if it doesn't work, put that idea aside and start again. Good design is all about trial and error!

# Resources

## SUPPLIERS

### UNITED KINGDOM

Actacrown Limited
Suite 6, 88–90 Hatton Garden
London
EC1N 8PN
(0)20 7404 1110

Cookson Precious Metals Ltd
59–83 Vittoria Street
Birmingham
B1 3NZ
www.cooksongold.com
(0)845 100 1122

The Bead Shop
21a Tower Street
London
WC2H 9NS
(0) 20 7240 0931
www.beadshop.co.uk

### UNITED STATES

Ackfeld Mfg.
P.O. Box 1268
Liberty, MO 64069
(888) 272-3135
www.ackfeldwire.com

Aldastar Corp.
70 Spruce St.
Paterson, NJ 07501
(973) 742-6787
www.aldastar.com

Artisan's Choice
2066 Wineridge Pl.
San Diego, CA 92029
(760) 480-0175
www.artisanschoice.com

Beadalon
205 Carter Dr.
West Chester, PA 19382
(610) 692-7551
www.beadalon.com

Beader's Paradise
4201 Guinn Rd.
Knoxville, TN 37031
(865) 927-3800

The Beadery
105 Canonchet Rd.

Hope Valley, RI 02832
(401) 539-2438
www.thebeadery.com

Beads World Inc.
1384 Broadway
New York, NY 10018
www.beadsworldusa.com

The Beadworks Group
www.beadworks.com

Black Hills Software
(Bead Wizard beading design
   software)
www.beadwizard.com

Cheep Trims
5524 Alcoa Ave.
Vernon, CA 90058
(877) BUY-TRIM
www.cheeptrims.com

Cottage Rose Collections
   (watch faces)
P.O. Box 32524
Tucson, AZ 85751
www.cottagerosecollec
   tions.com

Cousin Corp. of America
12333 Enterprise Blvd.
Largo, FL 33776
(727) 536-3568
www.cousin.com

The Craft Pedlars
1035 S. Shary Circle
Concord, CA 94518
(925) 837-1219
www.pedlars.com

Crafter's Pick
520 Cleveland Ave.
Albany, CA 94710
(510) 526-7616
www.crafterspick.com

Halcraft USA
30 W. 24th St., 9th floor
New York, NY 10010
(212) 376-1580
www.halcraft.com

Flights of Fancy
4005 Mesa Ridge Dr.
Fort Worth, TX 76137
(800) 530-8745
www.flightsoffancybou
   tique.com

Firefly Beadcrafts
12289 Windcliff Dr.
Davisburg, MI 48350
(248) 634-3649
www.fireflybead.com
GHI Inc.
305 Wildberry Ct., Ste. B-1
Schaumburg, IL 60193
(847) 891-5609
www.beadbuddy.net

Gold Crest
650 Ward Dr.
Santa Barbara, CA 93111
(800) 922-3233
www.goldcrestinc.com

Gutermann of America
8227 Arrowridge Blvd.
Charlotte, NC 28273
(704) 525-7068
www.gutermann.com

Hirschberg Schutz
650 Liberty Ave.
Union, NJ 07083
(908) 810-1111

Jesse James Button and Trim
615 N. New St.
Allentown, PA 18102
(610) 435-8254

Jewelcraft LLC
505 Windsor Dr.
Secaucus, NJ 07094
(201) 223-0804
www.jewelcraft.biz

Roylco, Inc.
3251 Abbeville Hwy.
Anderson, SC 29624
(800) 362-8656
www.roylco.com

Schylling
P.O. Box 513
Rowley, MA 01969
(978) 948-3601
www.schylling.com

### CANADA

John Bead Corp.
19 Bertrand Ave.
Toronto, ON M1L-2P3
(416) 757-3287
www.johnbead.com

Magenta
2275 Bombardier
Sainte-Julie, QB J3E-2J9
(450) 922-5253
www.magentastyle.com

Reiner Craft Corp.
765 Beaubien St. E, #108
Montreal, QB H25-1S8
(514) 324-8645
www.reinercraft.com

### INTERNATIONAL

Bead Shop
www.beadworks.co.uk

The Bead Shop
4114 N. Oakland Ave.
Milwaukee, WI 53211
(414) 961-9200
www.mailorder-beads.co.uk

The Bead Merchant
www.beadmerchant.co.uk

Celia's Vintage Clothing
www.celias-nottm.co.uk

# ASSOCIATIONS

## UNITED KINGDOM

The Bead Society of Great
  Britain
www.beadsociety.org.uk

## UNITED STATES

American Craft Council
21 S. Eltings Corner Rd.
Highland, NY 12528
(800) 836-3470
www.craftcouncil.org

Arts and Crafts Association of
  America
4888 Cannon Woods Ct.
Belmont, MI 49306
(616) 874-1721
www.artsandcraftsassoc.com

Association of Crafts &
  Creative Industries
1100-H Brandywine Blvd.
P.O. Box 3388
Zanesville, OH 43702
(740) 452-4541
www.accicrafts.org

Hobby Industry Association
319 E. 54th St.
Elmwood Park, NJ 07407
(201) 794-1133
www.hobby.org

National Craft Association
1945 E. Ridge Rd., Suite 5178
Rochester, NY 14622
(800) 715-9594

## CANADA

Canada Craft and Hobby
  Association
#24 1410-40 Ave., N.E.
Calgary, AL T2E 6L1
(403) 291-0559

Canadian Crafts Federation
c/o Ontario Crafts Council
Designers Walk
170 Bedford Rd., Suite 300
Toronto, ON M5R 2K9
(416) 408-2294
www.canadiancraftsfederation.ca

## Acknowledgements

There are lots of wonderful people who inspired, encouraged, and assisted me through this book, I really couldn't have done it without you, so my heartfelt thanks to:

Ma for writing me books when I was little, you always inspire me. Dad who keeps exciting findings to make fishing flies with and taught me a reef knot. Sister Roz always the prettiest and most enthusiastic recipient of my trial pieces. Husband Nik who actually encourages me to buy more beads! Simon Clay for the gorgeous photographs. Josephine Lanning, a wonderful and patient hand model. Rebekah Roberts, my sorcerer's apprentice who beaded as if her life depended on it. Liz Johnson, my fabulous personal bead shopper. All at The Bead Shop for beading madness and fun. Celia, Denise, Isabelle, Jets, Lynne, and Pauline for loaning me their marvellous bead work, you're all so talented. Frank Hopkinson and all at Anova Books for their support.